What we obtain too cheaply, we esteem too lightly. It is dearness only that gives everything its value. Heaven knows how to put a proper price upon its goods.

Thomas Paine

JOSEPH FIELDING McCONKIE

SEEKING THE SPIRIT

Deseret Book Company   Salt Lake City, Utah   1981

Library of Congress Cataloging-in-Publication Data

McConkie, Joseph F.
  Seeking the spirit.

  Includes index.
  1. Spiritual life—Mormon authors.
  2. Revelation (Mormonism) I. Title.
  BX8656.M28   248'.2   78-13372
  ISBN 0-87747-721-3 (hardbound)
  ISBN 1-57345-324-2 (paperbound)

Printed in the United States of America   72082

10 9   8   7   6   5   4   3   2   1

CONTENTS

ACKNOWLEDGMENTS

Special appreciation is extended to James A. Moss,
a colleague at the Brigham Young University,
and my brother Mark for their helpful suggestions
in the preparation of this work.
Appreciation is also extended to my father,
Elder Bruce R. McConkie, for his genial counsel
and encouragement.

PREFACE

*What we obtain too cheaply, we
esteem too lightly. It is dearness
only that gives everything its value.
Heaven knows how to put a proper
price upon its goods.*
Thomas Paine

In a conversation with Brigham Young, a man of science desirous of illustrating the ignorance of the Mormon elder asked how many elements there were. Brigham Young responded that neither of them knew, and suggested that the difference between them was that the antagonist ignorantly supposed that he did. In like manner it could appropriately be observed at the outset of this short volume that our knowledge of the many operations of the Spirit is at best limited. Illustrating this principle Joseph Smith said:

"We consider that God has created man with a mind capable of instruction, and a faculty which may be enlarged in proportion to the heed and diligence given to the light communicated from heaven to the intellect; and that the nearer man approaches perfection, the clearer are his views, and the greater his enjoyments, till he has overcome the evils of his life and lost every desire for sin; and like the ancients, arrives at that point of faith where he is wrapped in the power and glory of his Maker, and is caught up to dwell with Him. But we consider that this is a station to which no man ever arrived in a moment: he must have been instructed in the government and laws of that kingdom by proper degrees, until his mind is capable in some measure of comprehending the propriety, justice, equality, and consistency of the same." (*History of the Church* 2:8.)

Even the Savior did not attempt to define the process of spiritual growth. Rather, he said, "The wind bloweth where it listeth, and thou hearest the sound thereof, but canst not tell whence it cometh, and whither it goeth: so is everyone that is born of the Spirit." (John 3:8.) Though we cannot see the wind, we can hear it whistle and sing, and we can feel it pushing at our backs, or nipping and biting at our faces; still we know not "whence it cometh, and whither it goeth." Such was Christ's description of the sources of spiritual promptings. We feel them pushing at our backs, or when in error we experience their stinging bite, yet we do not fully understand where they came from nor do we fully realize where they will lead us. "As thou knowest not what is the way of the spirit," we read in Ecclesiastes, "nor how the bones do grow in the womb of her that is with child: even so thou knowest not the works of God who maketh all." (Ecclesiastes 11:5.) As has been frequently observed, the ability to define and explain is not necessary in order to experience and know.

Thus it is that as we struggle to climb the mountain of faith and view the world from its lofty vantage points, we are awed by what we see and humbled by the prospect of what lies ahead as we continue on to yet another plateau. Hopefully this little work will be helpful to at least a few as they pursue that journey.

CAN I REALLY KNOW?

And it came to pass
when they heard this voice,
and beheld that it was not a voice of thunder,
neither was it a voice of a great tumultuous noise,
but behold, it was
a still voice of perfect mildness,
as if it had been a whisper,
and it did pierce even to the very soul.
(Helaman 5:30.)

Two assumptions underlie all that is found within the covers of this book: first, that we can know the reality of God; and second, that to some degree we already know of that reality even though our present awareness may be very dim. Though it seems an awkward statement, we know more than we know we know. As Amulek testified, "I knew concerning these things, yet I would not know. . . ." (Alma 10:6.) It was Brigham Young who said that the truth of every revelation was independent within that revelation. (*JD* 9:149.) President Marion G. Romney explained that no one is justified in rejecting the teachings of the gospel of Jesus Christ "on the basis that he does not know they are true, because everything the Lord does or says has within itself the evidence of its own authenticity, and every person is divinely endowed with the means to discover that evidence and know for himself that it is true." (*CR*, April 1976, pp. 120-21.) Christ himself so testified:

"And he said also to the people, When ye see a cloud rise out of the west, straightway ye say, There cometh a shower; and so it is.

"And when ye see the south wind blow, ye say, There will be heat; and it cometh to pass.

"Ye hypocrites, ye can discern the face of the sky and of the earth; but how is it that ye do not discern this time?

1

"Yea, and why even of yourselves judge ye not what is right?" (Luke 12:54-57.)

Reminding his listeners that by reading the signs they could anticipate the weather, Jesus asked why they refused to be equally discerning about the signs of the times. He reasoned that even if they could not read the signs of the times, if they would only listen to the light within their souls they would know that he was the promised Messiah.

All are born into this world with the light of Christ. (D&C 84:46.) This light serves as a personal compass so that we might know, as Moroni said, with a "perfect knowledge" the course we should pursue. (Moroni 7:15-16.) Were it not for this light granted to all men, a just God could not hold them accountable for their actions, for knowledge must precede accountability. The very fact that God holds men accountable for their actions evidences to us that men have innately within them the capacity to distinguish between good and evil, between truth and error. For instance, Paul said that the "Gentiles, which have not the law, do by nature the things contained in the law. . . ." The works of the law, he explained, are "written in their hearts"; thus their "conscience" directs their course. (Romans 2:14-15.)

All men have an inborn propensity to worship God, to accept truth, and to live righteously; this innate desire has been variously referred to as the spirit of truth, the light of Christ, our conscience, or, as President Kimball called it, a "personal Liahona." (CR, October 1976, pp. 116-17.) The nature of these yearnings is to draw men closer and closer to the source of light. In so responding they are led to the gospel message and to embrace the new and everlasting covenant. (D&C 84:46-48.) Elaborating upon this principle Brigham Young said:

"I do not believe for one moment that there has been a man or woman upon the face of the earth, from the days of Adam to this day, who has not been enlightened, instructed and taught by the revelations of Jesus Christ. 'What! the ignorant heathen?' Yes, every human being who has possessed a sane mind. I am far from believing that the children of men have been deprived of the privilege of receiving the Spirit of the Lord to teach them right from wrong. No matter what the traditions of their fathers were, those who were honest before the Lord, and acted uprightly, according to the best knowledge they had, will have an opportunity to go into the kingdom of God. I believe this privilege belonged to the sons and daughters of Adam, and descended from him, and his children who were contemporary with him, throughout all generations." (*JD* 2:139.)

If by conversion we have reference to the adopting or accepting of new opinions or beliefs, there are relatively few converts in the Church. Many have converted in the sense that they have turned to righteousness and faith, but comparatively few declare a change in personal views or ideologies. Their feelings are more accurately described as an awakening of the memories of the spirit. Their so-called conversion does not consist as much in changing as it does in identifying or clarifying feelings or senses that were always theirs.

Few people, for instance, view God as a gaseous essence that fills the immensity of space, though he is so defined by all creedal religions. When the missionaries teach of a God who is a corporeal being; one who has body, parts, and passions; a loving Father in whose image they were literally created—they invariably respond, "Well, I always believed that!" And of course they did, even though it varies radically from the dogma of their churches.

It is significant that in our missionary lessons we assume no obligation to prove the existence of God. Might we ask, By what justification do we just assume the very foundation upon which all that we teach rests? The answer is simple: innate within every soul is the knowledge that God lives. That sure knowledge was shared by all prior to this life, and though our memories are dulled or dimmed with birth and must again be awakened, that knowledge and those feelings are the natural inheritance of every soul that comes into this life.

Some of the early members of the Church were quick to notice Joseph Smith's imperfections and thus question his prophetic calling. The Prophet's exposure to formal education had been very limited, and some of his more educated followers thought themselves better qualified than he to give written expressions to the revelations. The Lord, who knows the hearts and minds of all men, spoke to these self-supposing wise men, saying: "Your eyes have been upon my servant Joseph Smith,

Jun., and his language you have known, and his imperfections you have known; and you have sought in your hearts knowledge that you might express beyond his language; this you also know." (D&C 67:5.) The Lord challenged them to find the least of the revelations given to Joseph Smith and to appoint the wisest of their number to write one equal to it. Extending the challenge, the Lord invited any of their number who thought they could "make one like unto it" to do so. Should they succeed, the Lord said that they would then be justified in saying that they did not know the revelations were true. But if they failed, they would be under condemnation if they did not bear testimony to the truthfulness of the revelations received through Joseph Smith. (D&C 67:6-8.)

The Lord has not revoked the challenge. Any persons today who doubt the prophetic calling of the Prophet Joseph Smith (or question the existence of their own testimony of Joseph Smith) are invited to match his works, with the Lord's assurance that if they can, they are justified in retaining their doubt. But if they cannot match the works of the world's most prolific prophet, then they are "under condemnation" if they do not bear witness to the truthfulness of these things.

Significantly, it is in the actual bearing of testimony that the Spirit of the Lord most frequently settles upon a person, giving one an assurance of the verity of his own words. As the seed produces the flower, so the bearing of testimony results in testimony. Brigham Young illustrated this principle with the following story:

"One of our Elders with whom I was acquainted, after he was baptised, got cornered up, and was obliged to preach a sermon. He never had been able to say that he knew Joseph was a Prophet; but he was there in the meeting: the house was crowded with the congregation; the windows and doors full of people, and all around on the green waiting to hear a 'Mormon' preacher. There were none there but this one man, and he was called upon to preach. He thought he would pray and dismiss the meeting. He never had known that Joseph Smith was a Prophet: that was the lion that lay in his path; and he could not get by him, nor round about him, nor dig under him, nor leap over him; and the lion he must meet: he must say Joseph, for

4

better or worse. As soon as he got 'Joseph' out, 'is a Prophet' was the next; and from that, his tongue was loosened, and he continued talking until near sundown. The Lord pours out his Spirit upon a man when he testifies that which the Lord gives him to testify of. From that day to this, he has never been at a loss to know that Joseph was a Prophet." (*JD* 6:280.)

The Lord has spoken to many who have not heard. An interesting illustration of this principle is the story of Oliver Cowdery's conversion. While teaching school in Palmyra, he learned about the work of translation in which Joseph Smith was then engaged. By this time Joseph and his wife Emma had been forced to flee to Harmony, Pennsylvania, in order to escape the continued attempts to interrupt the work and steal the plates.

Having learned of the matter, Oliver found himself reflecting on it again and again. He felt impressed that he would have the privilege of writing for Joseph and finally he resolved to go to Harmony and offer his services. (*History of Joseph Smith, by His Mother,* p. 139.) His offer to help was gratefully accepted by Joseph Smith, and in a matter of days after his arrival, Oliver was busy recording the Prophet's words. At Oliver's request Joseph inquired of the Lord in his behalf. Responding to Oliver's plea for assurance, the Lord said: "Blessed art thou for what thou hast done; for thou hast inquired of me, and behold, as often as thou hast inquired thou hast received instruction of my Spirit." (D&C 6:14.)

Thus Oliver received a revelation, the primary purpose of which was to assure him that he had already been receiving revelation! As an evidence that he had been responding to the Spirit, the revelation continued, "If it had not been so, thou wouldst not have come to the place where thou art at this time."

Oliver had been responding to the promptings of the Spirit without realizing that he was doing so. By way of additional explanation the Lord said, "Thou knowest that thou hast inquired of me and I did enlighten thy mind; and now I tell thee these things that thou mayest know that thou hast been enlightened by the Spirit of truth." (D&C 6:15.) So that Oliver would be without reason to doubt this revelation, the Lord continued: "Verily, verily, I say unto you, if you desire a further witness, cast your mind upon the night that you cried unto me in your heart, that you might know concerning the truth of these things. Did I not speak peace to your mind?" Rhetorically the Lord then asked, "What greater witness can you have than from God?" (D&C 6:22-23.) By referring to this earlier experience, known only to Oliver, when he fervently sought the Lord in silent prayer and was encompassed in a spirit of peace, the Lord assured Oliver that Joseph Smith was indeed his mouthpiece, for Joseph could not have known these things except by revelation. Thus, Oliver gained the assurance that his prayers had been answered.

Like Oliver Cowdery, many of us desire some sort of heavenly manifestation to assure us that the course we are pursuing is approved of the Lord. As was the case with Oliver, the Lord has already spoken peace to our minds, enlightened our souls, and directed us to the place where we are at this time without our being fully sensitive to it.

Even when the gospel is taught with inspiration by a master teacher, many fail to recognize the promptings of the Spirit. The story in Luke about the two men traveling from Jerusalem to Emmaus provides an excellent illustration. As they pursued their journey, a distance of seven or eight miles, these two disciples conversed about the ministry of Christ, his crucifixion, and the reports of his resurrection. As they talked together, "Jesus himself drew near, and went with them." Retaining his glory within himself so they would not know him as he walked with them, "and beginning at Moses and all the prophets, he expounded unto them in all the scriptures the things concerning himself." (Luke 24:13-27.)

Imagine what a remarkable experience that would have been—to have God himself, the author of the scriptures, as one's own personal tutor! No two men ever had a more capable or competent teacher. Yet, while he was teaching them they had no realization of the greatness of the experience that was theirs. It was only at their journey's end, when they sat to eat and Christ broke bread and blessed it, that their "eyes were opened, and they knew him." Only then did the one turn to the other and say, "Did not our heart burn within us, while he talked with us by the way, and while he opened to us the scriptures?" (Luke 24:31-32.)

As is so often the case, the spiritual hindsight of these two disciples was appreciably better than their immediate spiritual insight. Their experience on the Emmaus road was such a natural one that they were not aware of the quiet and unobtrusive operations of the Spirit. It could be said of them as Christ said of the Lamanites converted by Ammon and his brothers: they were "baptized with fire and with the Holy Ghost, and they knew it not." (3 Nephi 9:20.)

The scriptures refer to the knowledge of the things of God as "hidden treasures." (D&C 89:19.) Implicit within this phrase are two concepts: first, that the knowledge of the things of the Spirit are not immediately apparent, but are hidden to those who will not search for them; and second, that once they have been found they will be of great worth.

Paul used the expression "hidden wisdom" to describe the gospel of Jesus Christ. (1 Corinthians 2:7.) Gospel principles, he explained, could not be known and understood in the same manner that we gain mastery of earthly or mundane things. The knowledge of spiritual things can only be taught and learned by the Spirit. "But the natural man receiveth not the things of the Spirit of God," he said, "for they are foolishness unto him: neither can he know them, because they are spiritually discerned." (1 Corinthians 2:14.)

Considerable effort is necessary to become fluent in the language of the Spirit. Some who are unwilling to expend the effort to learn that language justify their spiritual lethargy by denying the reality of such things. To all such, gospel treasures or wisdom remain hidden. Their ignorance of these truths no more negates their reality than that of a blind man denying the existence of light threatens the reality of light, or a deaf man denying the existence of sound threatens the reality of sound. Thus Paul declared:

"But as it is written, Eye hath not seen, nor ear heard, neither have entered into the heart of man, the things which God hath prepared for them that love him.

"But God hath revealed them unto us by his Spirit: for the Spirit searcheth all things, yea, the deep things of God.

"For what man knoweth the things of a man, save the spirit of man which is in him? even so the things of God knoweth no man, but the Spirit of God.

"Now we have received, not the spirit of the world, but the spirit which is of God; that we might know the things that are freely given to us of God.

"Which things also we speak, not in the words which man's wisdom teacheth, but which the Holy Ghost teacheth; comparing spiritual things with spiritual." (1 Corinthians 2:9-13.)

If we are to find the things of the Spirit, we must search in the realm of the Spirit. True religion can come from no other source. All true religion centers in feelings, and since feelings are not subject to a system of weights and measures, it is difficult to describe them to the unspiritual. Again our inability to describe those feelings doesn't negate their reality. An infant's ability to sense and feel the reality of parental love is not conditioned on his ability to explain those feelings. To know truth by sense and feeling without being able to explain or rationally defend it is an experience common to all mankind.

The essence of our testimony, which finds its roots in personal revelation, embraces the reality of God, the Church, and living prophets. In bearing that testimony we assume no obligation of proof. In the payment of debts I assume no obligation to prove that the money I offer "in good faith is genuine; you may believe it is counterfeit and refuse to accept it, but if you do, it is entirely up to you to prove your case or perhaps face a libel suit." (Hugh Nibley, *An Approach to the Book of Mormon,* p. 11.) To prove the reality of any truth to someone who does not want to accept it is a rather fruitless endeavor. The scribes, Sadducees, and Pharisees of old constantly taunted Jesus for proof, and when it was set before them in overwhelming abundance they continued to disbelieve it. Challenged to show proof, Christ said to his antagonists, "When it is evening, ye say, It will be fair weather: for the sky is red. And in the morning, It will be foul weather to day: for the sky is red and lowring. O ye hypocrites, ye can discern the face of the sky; but can ye not discern the signs of the times?" (Matthew 16:2-3.) "When a man asks for proof we can be pretty sure that proof is the last thing in the world he really wants." (Nibley, *op cit.,* p. 2.)

Our primary responsibility is to learn the gospel and follow it. Even in the context of missionary work we assume no obligation to answer every question or objection that might be raised. Sooner or later every man is backed up to the wall of faith where he must make his stand. (Ezra Taft Benson, *CR*, April 1975, p. 95.) God has never assumed the obligation to answer all our questions or tell us all he knows. Certainly we need not assume that responsibility as we act as his agents.

Not infrequently it is argued that in the process of investigating the gospel one might convince himself that it is true rather than actually receive an independent witness by the Spirit of its validity. Usually such arguments center in the suggestion that conversion is merely a response to a personal need to believe.

In the context of such a question it should be noted that essential elements of the need to believe are not different from the essential elements of the need to not believe held by disbelievers. After all, there are no beliefs or disbeliefs that are not at least partly determined by need. Disbelief is just as subject to personal need as any other position that a person might assume. It is just as easy for a person to fool himself into disbelief as it is for one to fool himself into belief. Nor is there any justification for associating a negative connotation with the need to believe. Quite to the contrary, such needs are inborn, having originated in the heavens.

When bearing testimony to a group of modern-day Pharisees, I was interrupted with the announcement that "they do not want to hear about those things that make you feel good!" Well, what kind of a religion is it that does not have within it the power to make you feel good? Apparently these people had a need for a religion that did not give them a good feeling, but certainly their rather peculiar need does not strip my belief of the cloth of truth.

There is no empty space. The Spirit of the Lord pervades all things. Brigham Young said that he would gladly pay for information as to where God was not. There is a fortune to be made, he reasoned, in selling such information to the wicked— thus granting them a place to hide from the wrath of God. (*JD* 3:279.)

Though God is "in all things, and is through all things, and is round about all things," there are obviously some places in which his Spirit is more abundantly available and more easily found than others. It is an uncomfortable experience to visit in a home where there is discord, fighting, and ugliness. Surely the Spirit of the Lord would be as anxious to excuse himself from such an environment as we are. We choose to associate with those among us with whom we feel most comfortable; the Spirit of the Lord does likewise.

A group of Church of Scotland ministers, angry about what they termed an "invasion" of Mormon missionaries into their country, challenged the mission president with the question, "What right do the Mormons have in Scotland?" In response the mission president suggested it as his understanding that there were two powers or influences in the world and that all that represented goodness, brotherly kindness, benevolence, and like virtues came from one of those sources, namely, God. The ministers were asked if they agreed. Of course they did. Then he said, "It is also my understanding that bitterness, hatred, resentment, and like feelings come from the other source which is Satan. Would you agree?" Again they concurred. "Now, then," he continued, "if any of you have any of those feelings in your hearts toward me or the church I represent, where did you get them?" With considerable embarrassment they realized the source of their feelings of bitterness.

Moroni and his father, Mormon, taught that "all things which are good cometh of God; and that which is evil cometh of the devil. . . ." (Moroni 7:12.) Succinctly stated, light and darkness will never meet; Christ and Satan will never shake hands. It is really that simple. That which invites and persuades to do good is of God and that which entices to do evil is of Satan. Christ and Satan are avowed enemies—there is no common ground upon which they both can stand. Satan wages an unremitting and uncompromising war with all that is good, and none can avoid the fight. The Spirit of Christ is given to every man who comes into the world, that all might distinguish between the two forces. One discerns between these opposing powers with a simple test: that which invites us to do good and persuades us to believe in Christ "is sent forth by the power and gift of Christ," while that which "persuadeth men to do evil, and believe not in Christ, and deny him, and serve not God, then ye may know with a perfect knowledge it is of the devil. . . ." (Moroni 7:16-17.)

Just as you cannot get a cooling drink from ocean waters, you cannot expect to find the Spirit of the Lord in disobedience or among the disobedient. Nor would one wisely seek it among those who despise purity, eschew faith, mock belief, ridicule works of righteousness, violate covenants, or speak evil of the Lord's anointed.

The Lord has declared, "If you keep not my commandments, the love of the Father shall not continue with you, therefore you shall walk in darkness." (D&C 95:12.) This principle is eternal and undeviating: "intelligence cleaveth unto intelligence; wisdom receiveth wisdom; truth embraceth truth; virtue loveth virtue; light cleaveth unto light; mercy hath compassion on mercy and claimeth her own; justice continueth its course and claimeth its own. . . ." (D&C 88:40.) All things produce after their own kind: the offspring of faith is faith, the offspring of disbelief is disbelief. "Draw near unto me and I will draw near unto you," the Lord has promised. (D&C 88:63.) "Seek me diligently and ye shall find me" is the promise granted to all. (D&C 88:63.)

The seed of faith has been planted within the souls of all the offspring of God. Warmed by the light of Christ, the seed swells and sprouts. Nurtured by works of righteousness, protected from the weeds of disbelief, and sustained with patience, the plant begins to grow with quiet grace. Almost immediately it enlarges the soul and enlightens the understanding. Properly nourished it takes root and, in Alma's language, becomes "a tree springing up unto everlasting life." (Alma 32:26-41.)

It is in the soil of life that the roots of faith must grow. The life of the tree and its fruits give evidence of its roots. Though unseen and unmeasured, they are the source of strength in storms and of nourishment for growth.

MANIFESTATION OR CONFIRMATION?

There is but one path of safety
to the Latter-day Saints,
and that is the path of duty.
It is not a testimony;
it is not a marvelous manifestation,
it is not knowing that the Gospel is true—
it is not actually knowing
that the Savior is the Redeemer;
but it is the keeping
of the commandments of God,
living the life of a Latter-day Saint.
(Heber J. Grant.)

God does not grant spiritual manifestations to gratify curiosity. Wilford Woodruff told of an occasion when one of the Council of the Twelve came to him and said, "I have prayed for a long time for the Lord to send me the administration of an angel. I have had a great desire for this, but I have never had my prayers answered." Elder Woodruff, who had had many such experiences, explained that if this man "were to pray a thousand years to the God of Israel for that gift, it would not be granted unless the Lord had a motive in sending an angel to him. I told him that the Lord never did nor never will send an angel to anybody merely to gratify the desire of the individual to see an angel." Surely the work of angels is greater than that of satisfying idle curiosity; nor are they the companions of the spiritually indigent. Wilford Woodruff explained that "if the Lord sends an angel to anyone, He sends him to perform a work that cannot be performed only by the administration of an angel." (*Deseret Weekly*, November 7, 1896.)

"Show me Latter-day Saints," said Joseph F. Smith, "who have to feed upon miracles, signs and visions in order to keep them steadfast in the Church, and I will show you members of the Church who are not in good standing before God, and who are walking in slippery paths. It is not by marvelous manifestations unto us that we shall be established in the truth, but it is by humility and faithful obedience to the commandments and laws of God." (*Gospel Doctrine*, p. 7.)

Spiritual experiences are granted to those who have merited the right to receive them. Stewardship of sacred treasures is granted only to trusted servants. We are reminded by way of revelation that "that which cometh from above is sacred, and must be spoken with care, and by constraint of the Spirit. . . ." (D&C 63:64.) Certainly the same standard applies in the dispensing of such things. It was the Master himself who admonished that we "Give not that which is holy unto the dogs, neither cast ye your pearls before swine. . . ." (Matthew 7:6.) Alma gave a perfect expression of this principle in these words: "It is given unto many to know the mysteries of God; nevertheless they are laid under a strict command that they shall not impart only according to the portion of his word which he doth grant unto the children of men, according to the heed and diligence which they give unto him." (Alma 12:9.)

Christ appeared to many after his resurrection. Paul tells us that he appeared to more than "five hundred brethren at once." (1 Corinthians 15:6.) Significantly, that number did not include unbelievers. Moroni explained that "it was by faith that Christ showed himself unto our fathers, after he had risen from the dead; and he showed not himself unto them until after they had faith in him; wherefore, it must needs be that some had faith in him, for he showed himself not unto the world." (Ether 12:7.) Often we can learn as much from what Christ did not do as we can from what he did. What he did not do was return to the Sanhedrin, where the great debate had raged over his testimony and works. He did not return to Caiaphas, to Pilate, to Herod, to the scribes, the Sadduccees, or the Pharisees, to manifest himself and prove them wrong. Conversion and faith do not grow out of such experiences, and the God of heaven has not chosen to so indulge the wicked. What he did was to return to those who believed, fulfilling the promise that signs would follow their good works.

It is a "wicked and adulterous generation," Christ declared, that "seeketh after a sign." (Matthew 16:4.) Joseph Smith said that it was made known to him by revelation that the Savior's statement was to be understood literally: when someone came forth seeking a sign, we could know with assurity that he had partaken of the spirit of lust and was guilty of adultery. To illustrate his point, Joseph Smith told of a meeting in which he was speaking at which a man interrupted demanding a sign. Pointing to the sign-seeker, the Prophet said, "That man is an adulterer." Another man in the crowd spoke up and said, "It is true, for I caught him in the very act." Later the man repented, confessed his adultery and was baptized into the Church. (*HC* 5:268.)

George A. Smith, one of the early leaders in the Church and a counselor to Brigham Young, told the following interesting story:

"When the Church of Jesus Christ of Latter-day Saints was first founded, you could see persons rise up and ask, 'What sign will you show us that we may be made to believe?' I recollect a Campbellite preacher who came to Joseph Smith, I think his name was Hayden. He came in and made himself known to Joseph, and said that he had come a considerable distance to be convinced of the truth. 'Why,' said he, 'Mr. Smith, I want to know the truth, and when I am convinced, I will spend all my talents and time in defending and spreading the doctrines of your religion, and I will give you to understand that to convince me is equivalent to convincing all my society, amounting to several hundreds.' Well, Joseph commenced laying before him the coming forth of the work, and the first principles of the Gospel, when Mr. Hayden exclaimed, 'O this is not the evidence I want, the evidence that I wish to have is a notable miracle; I want to see some powerful manifestation of the power of God, I want to see a notable miracle performed; and if you perform such a one, then I will believe with all my heart and soul, and will exert all my power and all my extensive influence to convince others; and if you will not perform a miracle of this kind, then I am your worst and bitterest enemy.' 'Well,' said Joseph, 'what will you have done? Will you be struck blind, or dumb? Will you be paralyzed, or will you have one hand withered?

Take your choice, choose which you please, and in the name of the Lord Jesus Christ it shall be done.' 'That is not the kind of miracle I want,' said the preacher. 'Then, sir,' replied Joseph, 'I can perform none, I am not going to bring any trouble upon any body else, sir, to convince you. I will tell you what you make me think of—the very first person who asked a sign of the Savior, for it is written, in the New Testament, that Satan came to the Savior in the desert, when he was hungry with forty days' fasting, and said, "If you be the Son of God, command these stones to be made bread." And now,' said Joseph, 'the children of the devil and his servants have been asking for signs ever since; and when the people in that day continued asking him for signs to prove the truth of the Gospel which he preached, the Savior replied, "It is a wicked and an adulterous generation that seeketh a sign." ' " (Brigham Young, *JD* 2:326-27.)

We have been directed to seek earnestly the best gifts. (D&C 46:8.) This process is one of faith and dedication. It is founded in righteous desires and an anxiety to be of greater service in the kingdom of God. Such a course stands in sharp contrast to the taunting spirit of those demanding proof before they will ascribe allegiance to the Lord's program. To such the Lord has said:

"Let the wicked take heed, and let the rebellious fear and tremble; and let the unbelieving hold their lips, for the day of wrath shall come upon them as a whirlwind, and all flesh shall know that I am God.

"And he that seeketh signs shall see signs, but not unto salvation.

"Verily, I say unto you, there are those among you who seek signs, and there have been such even from the beginning."

But such is not the source of faith, for the Lord explained, "faith cometh not by signs, but signs follow those that believe.

"Yea, signs come by faith, not by the will of men, nor as they please, but by the will of God.

"Yea, signs come by faith, unto mighty works, for without faith no man pleaseth God; and with whom God is angry he is not well pleased; wherefore, unto such he showeth no signs, only in wrath unto their condemnation." (D&C 63:6-11.)

To harvest the rich fruits of the gospel, one must first plant and nurture the seeds of faith. The law is eternal: "ye receive no witness until after the trial of your faith." (Ether 12:6.) God will not dishonor his own laws; faith must precede the miracle. If there is no faith, there can be no miracle. Conversely, if there is faith, signs of necessity must follow. Thus it has always been and thus it will always be; planting precedes harvesting, works precede assurance, confirmation precedes manifestation. Few plants grow to maturity overnight. The process is gradual, almost imperceptible. The same is true of spiritual growth. Joseph F. Smith described it thus:

"When I as a boy first started out in the ministry, I would frequently go out and ask the Lord to show me some marvelous thing, in order that I might receive a testimony. But the Lord withheld marvels from me, and showed me the truth, line upon line, precept upon precept, here a little and there a little, until he made me to know the truth from the crown of my head to the soles of my feet, and until doubt and fear had been absolutely purged from me. He did not have to send an angel from the heavens to do this, nor did he have to speak with the trump of an archangel. By the whisperings of the still small voice of the Spirit of the living God, he gave to me the testimony I possess. And by this principle and power he will give to all the children of men a knowledge of the truth that will stay with them, and it will make them to know the truth, as God knows it, and to do the will of the Father as Christ does it. And no amount of marvelous manifestations will ever accomplish this. It is obedience, humility, and submission to the requirements of heaven and to the order established in the kingdom of God upon the earth, that will establish men in the truth. Men may receive the visitation of angels; they may speak in tongues; they may heal the sick by the laying on of hands; they may have visions and dreams; but except they are faithful and pure in heart, they become an easy prey to the adversary of their souls, and he will lead them into darkness and unbelief more easily than others." (*Gospel Doctrine*, p. 7.)

David O. McKay spoke of struggles with similar feelings. As a young man he too had the idea that he did not have a testimony unless he had an experience like that of Joseph Smith in the Sacred Grove, or like his father, who had the voice of the

Lord speak to him. Sensing that nothing would be of greater worth to him than a testimony, David O. McKay prayerfully sought it. "I remember," he said, "riding over the hills one afternoon, thinking of these things, and concluded that there in the silence of the hills was the best place to get that testimony. I stopped my horse, threw the reins over his head, withdrew just a few steps and knelt by the side of a tree.

"The air was clear and pure, the sunshine delightful; the verdure of the wild trees and grass and the flowers scented the air; as I recall the incident now, all the surroundings come to me anew. I knelt down and with all the fervor of my heart poured out my soul to God and asked him for a testimony of this gospel. I had in mind that there would be some manifestation, that I should receive some transformation that would leave me without doubt.

"I arose, mounted my horse, and as he started over the trail I remember rather introspectively searching myself, and involuntarily shaking my head, said to myself, 'No sir, there is no change; I am just the same boy I was before I knelt down.' The anticipated manifestation had not come.

"Nor was that the only occasion. However, it did come, but not in the way I had anticipated. Even the manifestation of God's power and presence of his angels came, but when it did come, it was simply a confirmation; it was not a testimony."

President McKay testified that the witness that he sought came but not in the way he had anticipated. As a young missionary in Scotland he received one of many subsequent confirmations. It was at a priesthood meeting in which a man stood and said, "Brethren, there are angels in this room!" President McKay observed that the declaration did not impress him very much, but that the Spirit present did impress him. At that point President James L. McMurrin arose and said, "Yes, there are angels in this room," and then commenced to make a number of prophetic statements. Turning to Elder McKay, he paraphrased the words of the Savior to Peter, saying, "Let me say to you, Brother David, Satan hath desired you that he may sift you as wheat, but God is mindful of you." Then he added, "If you will keep the faith, you will yet sit in the leading councils of the Church."

President McKay said, "I knew that the answer to my boy-ish prayer had come." With inspired insight he added, "But the testimony that this work is divine had come, not through manifestation, great and glorious as it was, but through obedience to God's will, in harmony with Christ's promise, 'If any man will do his will, he shall know of the doctrine, whether it be of God, or whether I speak of myself.'" (John 7:17.) (*Improvement Era*, September 1962, pp. 628-29.)

Perhaps the most frequently used illustration of individual responsibility in the process of receiving revelation is Oliver Cowdery's attempt to translate the plates from which we re-ceived the Book of Mormon. Oliver had received the promise of the Lord that he could translate. He believed that promise. There was no reason to suppose that the Spirit of the Lord would not bless him in his efforts as a translator. Yet Oliver had not fully understood the operations of the Spirit, and to his own great surprise, he discovered that despite the Lord's promise he did not have the ability to translate. Frustrated, he asked Joseph Smith to inquire of the Lord as to why his efforts had failed. In response, the Lord told Oliver that he had not understood, for he had supposed that answers would be given for the asking. Such is not the system of heaven. "You must study it out in your mind," Oliver was told, and when you feel that you have solved the matter, then you must ask, and if your solution is correct, the Lord said, "I will cause that your bosom shall burn within you; therefore, you shall feel that it is right." (D&C 9:8.)

To that point Oliver had not fully appreciated the effort necessary on Joseph's part to translate, nor had he realized that the Lord expects us to use every facility at our command to solve problems and get answers before he will give his confirma-tion. It was further explained to Oliver that if his conclusions were not right, he would not receive the burning in his bosom, but would experience a "stupor of thought" that would cause him to forget that which was wrong. (D&C 9:9.)

Like tempered steel, correct principles hold their shape—they are not bent or twisted by circumstances. Thus it is that we find the brother of Jared learning that an individual's responsi-bility to research and study a matter out is as applicable to the building of ships as it is to the translating of ancient records.

Having built the barges as he had been commanded, the brother of Jared went to the Lord with two problems: the matter of lighting them and the problem of obtaining fresh air. Because the matter of obtaining fresh air was beyond man's experience, the Lord freely responded with instructions on this matter; however, the Lord made no response to the question about lighting the ship. Again the brother of Jared approached the Lord and asked his question. This time the Lord responded with a question of his own: "What will ye that I should do that ye may have light in your vessels?"

Then the brother of Jared realized that this was his problem; that the Lord would help, but the responsibility of at least recommending a solution was his. Clearly the Lord expected him to be as self-reliant as possible. After serious consideration, he determined upon a solution. He would molten out of rock sixteen small transparent stones. Stones in hand, he ascended the mountain, where he again sought the Lord and asked him to touch each of the stones with his finger that they might give light. Honoring the recommended solution of his servant, the Lord reached out and touched the stones one by one so that they would give forth light. (Ether 2:19-25; 3:1-6.)

Having reviewed these and like illustrations, Elder Bruce R. McConkie summarizes and defines the formula for receiving revelation: "If you learn how to use the agency that God has given you, and if you try to make your own decisions, and if you reach conclusions that are sound and right, and you counsel with the Lord and get his ratifying seal of approval upon the conclusions you've reached, then you've received revelation." (*BYU Speeches of the Year*, February 27, 1973.) More revelations come pursuant to this pattern than in any other manner.

A perfect illustration of the application of these principles was given to us by Heber J. Grant as he described the process in which the revelation on the welfare program was received. He reportedly said: "We had been meeting morning after morning for months, and we have evolved a plan. After we had evolved a plan I went especially in prayer to the Lord and prayed with all earnestness to know whether or not this plan met with His approval. In response there came over me, from the crown of my head to the soles of my feet such a sweet spirit and a burning within, that I knew God approved." (As quoted by William E. Berrett in an address to seminary and institute teachers, BYU, June 27, 1956.)

Spiritual strength is the natural result of spiritual labor. The system attests to the wisdom of God. We are granted that which we are ready to receive, that which we have the wisdom to understand, and the discretion to govern. The mansions of faith must be built brick by brick.

HOW CHRIST LEARNED
THE GOSPEL

Jesus, like all such Jewish lads,
was given the simple but effective home training
customary in his day.
The Scriptures being the only text-books,
their words formed
the material of education in the home.
The process of informing the mind with this material
began at an early age.
The zeal of parents in teaching
this sacred wisdom to their children
is well-known.
(Henry Kendall Booth.)

The Lord has never placed a premium on indolence or ignorance. This becomes evident as we examine the manner in which he has chosen to educate his prophets. Let us look first at the life of Christ, he being our exemplar and prototype in all things.

In its present form, the New Testament preserves only a faint outline of the early life and training of Christ. Of the Gospel writers, only Matthew and Luke recount the story of his nativity. Matthew tells of the angel of the Lord instructing Joseph to take Mary as his wife, of the visit of the wise men sometime after the birth of Christ, of the subsequent fleeing of the holy family into Egypt, of Herod's order to slaughter all the children in Bethlehem and its coasts, and then of the holy family's return to Nazareth. Luke recounts the story of John's birth, of Gabriel's announcement to Mary that she would be the mother of the Son of God, of Mary's visit to Elisabeth, of Mary and Joseph's journey to Bethlehem, of the birth of Christ, of the angelic chorus, of the visit of the shepherds, of Simeon's blessing the Christ child, and of the testimony of Anna.

By weaving these accounts together, we obtain the story of

23

Jesus' birth and an abbreviated account of the family experiences during the first two or three years of his life. From that point until Christ commenced his formal ministry, a period of perhaps twenty-seven or twenty-eight years, the Bible is nearly silent. Luke told us that the Christ "child grew, and waxed strong in spirit," that he was "filled with wisdom," and that "the grace of God was upon him." (Luke 2:40.) Luke then briefly told the story of Christ conversing with the doctors in the temple when twelve years of age. He concluded this story with the observation that Jesus "increased in wisdom and stature, and in favour with God and man." (Luke 2:41-52.) Nothing is said of the next eighteen years of Christ's life.

It is these lost years of Christ's life that we desire to reconstruct. If we can discover the manner in which he was prepared for the ministry, surely we will learn much as to how we should prepare for our own earthly missions. Caution is appropriate in such a journey, for as James E. Talmage pointed out, the inspired scribes treated the youth of Christ with "hallowed silence." For us to invent circumstances or to embellish the accounts given us, as, for instance, the Apocrypha writers did, brings no honor either to Christ or ourselves. (*Jesus the Christ*, p. 111.) We enter the sanctuary of those lost years only at the invitation of authoritative guides. Gratefully, we discover that if we are willing to properly prepare for the journey, our guides are willing to lead us further and show us more than is normally seen by the Sunday morning scriptural tourist.

Christ was born as are all children, helpless and dependent. Destined to ascend above all things, it was necessary that he first descend below them all. (D&C 122:8.) "I would believe that he was one of the weakest children that was ever born," said Brigham Young, "one of the most helpless at his birth; so helpless that it might have been supposed that he would never grow up to manhood." (*JD* 3:366.)

Christ was born in a hillside cave, possibly shared with beasts of the field, to a peasant girl and foster father. His beginnings were of all men most humble. He was born while his parents were traveling back to Bethlehem; the scriptural account does not tell us that there was no room in the inn, but rather it says there was no room "for them" in the inn. (Luke 2:7.) If

Mary was not about to give birth to a child, if they were not Galileans, whom the Judean Jews held in contempt, perhaps things would have been different. In the Inspired Version, Joseph Smith changed this verse to read "there was none to give room for them in the inns." Thus we learn that it was "the traveling hosts of Judah generally, not just an innkeeper or an isolated few persons, who withheld shelter from Joseph and Mary." (Bruce R. McConkie, *Doctrinal New Testament Commentary* 1:92.) Their rude rejection was but a prelude of that which was to come.

Surely Paul spoke literally when he said, "God hath chosen the weak things of the world to confound the things which are mighty; And base of the world . . . to bring to nought things that are: That no flesh should glory in his presence." (1 Corinthians 1:27-29.) Centuries before, Isaiah had depicted the youthful Christ as a "tender plant, and as a root out of a dry ground." Isaiah saw him then, not as a towering tree in a fertile forest, but as a lowly plant struggling to survive in arid soil. Of his physical appearance, Isaiah said, "He hath no form nor comeliness; and when we shall see him, there is no beauty that we should desire him." (Isaiah 53:2.)

As is the case with all men, Jesus' knowledge of the pre-earth life was taken from him when his spirit entered its mortal tabernacle. Nor was he to be spared the ailments, afflictions, or anguish that are the common lot of all mankind. Isaiah depicted him as being "despised and rejected of men; a man of sorrows, and acquainted with grief. . . ." (Isaiah 53:3.) Surely such expressions do not have exclusive reference to the days of his ministry. Should we naively suppose that his confrontation with Satan after his forty-day fast in the wilderness was the first occasion upon which the father of lies had attempted to divert him from his sacred calling?

As we reflect upon the manner in which Christ prepared for his ministry, should we assume that his visit to the temple when twelve years of age was the only occasion in his youth on which he entered its once sacred portals? Should we assume that that was the only occasion upon which he visited the Holy City, or conversed with the wise men, or spoke openly and publicly of gospel principles? Unless his life embraced the normal struggles of youth and the gradual process of assimilating knowledge and growing to maturity, it would be valueless as an example for the rest of mankind.

The most important characters and thus the most important teachers in the life of Christ were Joseph and Mary. The concept that parents are responsible to teach their children the gospel is not an addendum added in the latter days. It is the eternal order of things. Joseph was a visionary man, a man acquainted with the things of the spirit, a man who dreamed dreams, entertained angels, and who had full confidence in all instructions that came from the throne of God. He was exacting in his observance of the Mosiac law. He was, as Matthew tells us, "a just man." (Matthew 1:19.) Joseph's role was greater than that of merely teaching his sons a vocation. It takes little imagination to suppose that as they worked and while the family ate, he recited the stories of their ancestors, "a custom traditionally begun in the time of the Patriarch Abraham, some 2000 years earlier. Joseph also taught his son the duties required of every faithful Israelite." (*Great People of the Bible and How They Lived,* p. 324.)

At the day's end, Joseph would go to the synagogue for the evening meeting. Jesus and his brothers, as they came of age, would attend with him. Their conversations would center in the scriptures and the promises made to Israel. That Joseph was a man who knew the scriptures, loved the gospel, believed its promises, and directed the course of his family as an inspired patriarch is not open to question.

Mary, the mother of the Christ child, was known to and described by prophets centuries before her birth. Alma describes her as a "precious and chosen vessel." (Alma 7:10.) Nephi, who saw her in vision some six hundred years before the birth of her firstborn son, described her as being "exceedingly fair and white," a "virgin, most beautiful and fair above all other virgins." (1 Nephi 11:13, 15.) As there is only one Christ, so there is only one Mary. Of all the preexistent hosts, no woman was greater than she.

When Jesus was born, Mary "wrapped him in swaddling clothes and laid him in a manger." (Luke 2:7.) Thus it appears that the birth took place without the assistance of other persons. Joseph is not even mentioned here. So it was, in the raising of the Christ child, that there was that which Mary and Mary alone, with her mother's love, could accomplish. It was Mary herself who took the infant child and wrapped him up and laid him in the manger. Swaddling clothes were long strips of linen in which the child was bound so tightly that he could move neither arms nor legs. "This ancient custom was based on the belief that the child's limbs would not grow straight and strong unless they were bound so they could not move freely for at least six months." (*Great People of the Bible...*, p. 320.) Correct or not, the custom could be viewed as a symbol of the loving arms of this "precious and chosen vessel" who would shape the character of her infant son that it too might be "straight and strong."

It is significant that when Joseph and Mary returned to Jerusalem to find their twelve-year-old son, who was then capable of confounding the wisest of men, without objection he returned with them to Nazareth where he was "subject unto them." (Luke 2:51.) His life affords an appropriate example for all children in the manner in which he early rendered perfect filial duty to his parents. A significant addition to the lost years of Jesus' life is restored to us in the Inspired Version. In some verses added by the Prophet to the third chapter of Matthew we read "that Jesus grew up with his brethren" and that "he served under his father." (JST, Matthew 3:24-25.) As the oldest son in a large family, he would have learned to share and assume responsibility. He enjoyed the association of cousins, aunts, uncles, and perhaps that of grandparents. (Luke 2:44.)

Our knowledge of the Jewish culture at that time justifies the conclusion that he was "well taught in the law and the scriptures, for such was the rule." Those traditions required that he be "trained to labor, for idleness was abhorred" then, as it should be today; "and every Jewish boy, whether carpenter's son, peasant's child, or rabbi's heir, was required to learn and follow a practical and productive vocation." (James E. Talmage, *Jesus the Christ,* p. 112.) Jesus would have started school after his sixth birthday. Classes were held six days a week at the synagogue, with all male children being required to attend.

The proving and trials of Christ, as is the case with all young men, began long before his mission. Nothing could be more naive than to suppose that he grew to maturity in a vacuum untouched by pain, sorrow, suffering, or temptation.

Conceived "after the manner of the flesh" (1 Nephi 11:18), Christ "took not on him the nature of angels," Paul testified; rather "he took on him the seed of Abraham. Wherefore in all things it behoved him to be made like unto his brethren. . . . For in that he himself hath suffered being tempted, he is able to succour them that are tempted." (Hebrews 2:16-18.)

How meaningless Christ's example would be if he, too, was not subject "like unto his brethren" to all the wiles of the flesh. The promise that life would be easy has not been granted to any man. Christ was not spared any trials, frustrations, anguish, or hardships of youth. All were his, for such is the purpose of mortality. His experiences were human experiences; his lot, the common lot of all mankind; that to which we are subject, he was subject; that which we experience, Christ also experienced. (Hebrews 2:14.)

That he might one day succor those who suffered, he suffered; that he might strengthen those who were tempted, he was tempted. "For we have not an high priest which cannot be touched with the feeling of our infirmities. . . . For that he himself also is compassed with infirmity." (Hebrews 4:15; 5:2.) Thus Paul assures us that "though he were a Son, yet learned he obedience by the things which he suffered; And being made perfect, he became the author of eternal salvation unto all them that obey him." (Hebrews 5:8-9.)

The same principles are taught to us in the Book of Mormon by the prophet Alma. He wrote:

"And he shall go forth, suffering pains and afflictions and temptations of every kind; and this that the word might be fulfilled which saith he will take upon him the pains and the sicknesses of his people.

"And he will take upon him death, that he may loose the bands of death which bind his people; and he will take upon him their infirmities, that his bowels may be filled with mercy, according to the flesh, that he may know according to the flesh how to succor his people according to their infirmities.

"Now the Spirit knoweth all things; nevertheless the Son of God suffereth according to the flesh that he might take upon him the sins of his people, that he might blot out their transgressions according to the power of his deliverance; and now behold, this is the testimony which is in me. (Alma 7:11-13.)

Isaiah described Christ as "despised and rejected of men; a man of sorrows, and acquainted with grief"; despised, and esteemed not. (Isaiah 53:3.) Those feelings were not new to Christ when he commenced his mortal ministry, for the experiences of his youth had done much to steel him for that which was to come.

In addition to the statement by Luke that Jesus increased in wisdom and favor with God, we have the testimony of John the Baptist who said that he saw that Christ did not receive of the "fulness at the first, but received grace for grace; And he received not of the fulness at first, but continued from grace to grace, until he received a fulness; And thus he was called the Son of God, because he received not of the fulness at the first." (D&C 93:12-14.) Significantly, his advancement was from "one grace to another, not from gracelessness to grace"; it was from "good to greater good, not from evil to good; from favor with God to greater favor, not from estrangement because of sin to reconciliation through repentance and propitiation." (Talmage, *Jesus the Christ*, p. 112.)

Whether John's testimony that Christ advanced from grace to grace was obtained solely by revelation or whether it combines both revelatory experience with years of personal association, we cannot say with perfect assurance at present. But in either case, the conclusion is the same—Christ advanced in the things of the spirit as we are to advance, from grace to grace.

Christ declared that the "fulness of the scriptures" constituted the "key of knowledge." (JST, Luke 11:53.) During his ministry, the scriptures were a primary source of his teachings. Those questioning his claim as the promised Messiah were challenged to "search the scriptures" (John 5:39), for such a search would lead the sincere investigator to the knowledge that he was indeed the Christ. His scriptural mastery witnessed a youth well spent in profitable study. "It is repeatedly recorded in the Gospels, that he met the insolent superiority of scribe and rabbi by scripture quotations, prefaced by the question, 'Have ye never read?' " (Matthew 12:3; 19:4; 21:16; 22:31; Mark 2:25; Luke 6:3.) (Henry Kendall Booth, *The World of Jesus,* p. 35.) Luke informs us that the customary manner in which he taught the gospel was to go into the synogogues on the sabbath day where he would read and teach the scriptures. (Luke 4:16.)

To picture Jesus as "an uneducated and unlearned artisan, a sort of journeyman carpenter," who had been endowed with wisdom from on high, thus enabling him even at the age of twelve to confound the wisest of men, is to do him considerable injustice. As one author suggested, such a view is "too much like a hillbilly preacher who never finished grammar school standing up in a pulpit, opening the Bible at random, and, by sheer God-given inspiration, preaching a wonderful soul-saving sermon 'by the power of the Holy Spirit' which converts even the atheistic professors who drop in out of curiosity." (Charles Francis Potter, *The Lost Years of Jesus Revealed,* pp. 39-40.)

The Lord's directive to Hyrum Smith, that he not attempt to declare the gospel message until he had first sought to obtain it, held equal sway anciently. Christ obtained the "power of God unto the convincing of men" in the same manner as did Hyrum Smith—through proper preparation. (D&C 11:21-22.)

It is, in fact, a simple matter to determine how Christ learned the gospel and prepared for his ministry. We need simply see what he has asked us to do, and we will thereby have identified what he did. Since he has challenged us to search the scriptures, we know that he searched the scriptures; since he has challenged us to seek learning by "study and also by faith," we know that he sought learning in the same manner. Since he has challenged us to be conversant with "things both in heaven and in the earth, and under the earth; things which have been, things which are, things which must shortly come to pass; things which are at home, things which are abroad; the wars and the perplexities of the nations, and the judgments which are on the land; and a knowledge also of countries and of kingdoms" in order that we may be prepared to magnify our callings and the mission with which he commissioned us, can we not then suppose that he was equally well prepared? (D&C 88:79-80.)

The Jews who were constantly astonished at Christ's understanding asked, "How is it that this man has learning [is so versed in the sacred scripture and in theology] when he has never studied?" (See John 7:15.) True, Jesus was not trained as the rabbis were trained or as sectarian ministers are trained in this age. He was not a graduate of a theological seminary, nor were his teachings associated with academic credentials. His knowledge differed from that of man's, as the heavens differ from the earth. (Isaiah 55:8-9.)

In the Inspired Version account of his visit with the wise men in the temple, instead of our being told that his parents found him "sitting in the midst of the doctors, both hearing them, and asking them questions," we read that the doctors "were hearing *him*, and *asking him* questions." (JST, Luke 2:46. Italics added.) The idea that he went forth to teach and not to be taught (D&C 43:15) is also found in the Inspired Version, in which we read, "And he served under his father, and he spake not as other men, neither could he be taught; for he needed not that any man should teach him." (JST, Matthew 3:25.) Though his parents were master teachers and though he was a gifted student—one without peer—of the scriptures; and though he garnered knowledge by study, he gained the wisdom that saves by prayer, thought, and action. The ultimate source of his knowledge needed to be—as it must be for all men—revelation, for that is the foundation upon which the kingdom of God rests.

He too was schooled under the sometimes harsh schoolmaster of life. He too was subject to the unrelenting buffetings of Satan. His was not a private school. For where he walked we are invited to walk; what he saw, we are entitled to see; what he did, we too should do; as he was blessed, we will be blessed; as he was sustained in moments of trial, we will be sustained; and as he succeeded, we may succeed.

THE SPIRITUAL EDUCATION
OF JOSEPH SMITH

Behold, I am God
and have spoken it;
these commandments are of me,
and were given unto my servants
in their weakness,
after the manner of their language,
that they might come to understanding.
And inasmuch as they erred
it might be made known;
And inasmuch as they sought wisdom
they might be instructed;
And inasmuch as they sinned
they might be chastened, that they might repent;
And inasmuch as they were humble
they might be made strong,
and blessed from on high,
and receive knowledge from time to time.
(D&C 1:24-28.)

God calls and educates his own prophets. The idea is prevalent that with the call to the prophetic office comes an endowment of spiritual ability, understanding, and power that was not previously experienced and that exceeds that which is enjoyed generally by righteous men. Challenging that conclusion, Elder Bruce R. McConkie has written that a call to positions of leadership "adds little knowledge or power of discernment to an individual, although every person called to a position in the Church does grow in grace, knowledge, and power by magnifying the calling given him." (*Mormon Doctrine,* p. 309.)

Essentially, the matter in question is this: are prophets called to their office and then endowed with the necessary abilities to magnify it, or are they schooled for their office and then called to it? As we quickly scan the history of calls to prophetic office, we think of Moses and the burning bush; of Christ saying to Peter and the other apostles, "Follow me"; of Saul on the road to Damascus; of Joseph Smith in the Sacred Grove; but were these calls to serve or calls to prepare for service?

The fragmentary nature of our scriptural accounts preserves for us only the barest details on many matters of great interest. The spiritual training received by Moses for forty years at the hands of his father-in-law, Jethro, from whom he received the priesthood, must have been considerable. Through Joseph Smith we learn that before Moses returned to Egypt he was caught up onto a high mountain where he saw and conversed with God. This experience was followed by a personal confrontation with Satan. After commanding Satan to depart, Moses had the power of God rest upon him, thus enabling Moses to see every particle of the earth and all of its inhabitants. Suffice it to say his mission to Egypt was preceded by considerably more training than is generally supposed. (Moses 1.)

The three years of Christ's ministry in large measure were devoted to training the twelve so that they might direct the Church after his ascension. What training they received prior to their callings to follow Christ as apostles is, of course, unknown to us, but to suppose that they were first seasoned in the things of the kingdom as elders seems a natural assumption. As to Paul, we misunderstand his experience on the road to Damascus if we suppose that it constituted a call to serve. Paul was called to repent and directed to Damascus to wait upon the Lord. There, under the direction of Ananias, he would be baptized for the remission of sins and be carefully taught the gospel. His call to service was still yet future.

In like manner, the first vision did not give Joseph Smith authority over anyone. Like a patriarchal blessing, it represented a call to prepare rather than a call to step forth as a prophet to the people. It was to be another ten years before the Church was organized, at which time Joseph would be sustained to preside over five others. That interim period of time was one of intense preparation and testing. It was one in which Joseph Smith was tutored by angels and buffeted by devils. The experiences of those years were necessary to steel him for that which was to come and to lead him to the point where he would one day say,

"I am like a huge, rough stone rolling down from a high mountain; and the only polishing I get is when some corner gets rubbed off by coming in contact with something else, striking with accelerated force against religious bigotry, priestcraft, lawyer-craft, doctor-craft, lying editors, suborned judges and jurors, and the authority of perjured executives, backed by mobs, blasphemers, licentious and corrupt men and women—all hell knocking off a corner here and a corner there. Thus I will become a smooth and polished shaft in the quiver of the Almighty, who will give me dominion over all and every one of them, when their refuge of lies shall fail, and their hiding place shall be destroyed, while these smooth-polished stones with which I come in contact become marred." (*HC* 5:401.)

Since we can deal with the period of history in which Joseph Smith lived with greater accuracy than we can with past dispensations, let us trace his spiritual growth in search of conclusions that will have meaningful application in our own lives.

To the Prophet Joseph Smith the Lord said, "This generation [age or dispensation] shall have my word through you." (D&C 5:10.) The Prophet laid the theological foundations of Mormonism. He stands as this dispensation's greatest doctrinal teacher. He "has given to our present world more holy scripture than any single prophet who ever lived; indeed, he has preserved for us more of the mind and will and voice of the Lord than the total of the dozen most prolific prophetic penmen of the past." (Bruce R. McConkie, *CR*, April 1976, p. 142.)

Our question is, To what extent was Joseph Smith required to study, struggle, and ponder, in his search for understanding, and to what extent was he granted answers by inspiration or revelation? To answer this question, let us first review the experience that he had and the process that was involved in translating the Book of Mormon.

Though not highly educated, the family in which Joseph Smith grew up was hard working and intelligent. They shared a keen interest in spiritual things, prayed together, sang together, and read the Bible together. Nonetheless, Joseph's father, Joseph Smith, Sr., and his grandfather, Asael Smith, were regarded as religious rebels by their neighbors. Neither would join with the denominations of the day, being unable to reconcile the teachings of the churches with the scriptures or sound reasoning. Joseph Smith, Sr., contended for the "ancient order" established by Christ and his apostles. Asael prophetically declared that one of his descendants would promulgate a work that would "revolutionize the world of religious faith." (E. Cecil McGavin, *The Family of Joseph Smith,* p. 9.) Joseph, Sr., was a visionary man, who on several occasions dreamed dreams that directed him in his search for the truth prior to the restoration. (*History of Joseph Smith, by His Mother,* pp. 46-49, 64-66, 68.) Joseph's mother, Lucy Mack Smith, struggled with what she called "anxiety of mind" in her quest for religion. She recalled: "I spent much of my time reading the Bible and praying," but her search for a church was frustrating. If she remained a member of no church, she said, all religious people would say she was of the world, and if she joined one of the churches, all the rest would say she was in error. "No church will admit that I am right except the one with which I am associated. This makes them witnesses against each other, and how can I decide in such a case as this, seeing they are all unlike the Church of Christ, as it existed in former days!" (*History of Joseph Smith,* p. 31.) Unable to find the religion she sought, she determined to search the Bible, using Christ and his disciples as her guide. (Ibid., p. 36.)

Such was the setting in which Joseph Smith had planted within his own heart and soul the desire to seek after spiritual things. He had been taught to trust in the Lord, to be discerning, to ask questions, and to seek answers. In a recently found account of the first vision, he indicated that the search that led him to the Sacred Grove was preceded by three years of pondering, attending meetings, listening to others, and studying. (Dean C. Jessee, "The Early Accounts of Joseph Smith's First Vision," *BYU Studies,* Spring 1969, p. 279.)

It was not a passing whim that lead Joseph Smith to the Sacred Grove. Much preparation had preceded his date with destiny, and much preparation would yet follow before he would be entrusted with the keys of the kingdom of God and directed to organize that kingdom again upon the earth.

Joseph never explained the manner in which he translated the Book of Mormon. On one occasion his brother Hyrum called on him in a public meeting to tell how the work was accomplished. In response, Joseph said that it was "not intended to tell the world all the particulars of the coming forth of the Book of Mormon," and that "it was not expedient" for him to relate such things. (*HC* 1:220.)

Because the details of the work of translation have not been entrusted to us, some explanations have been offered that are clearly contrary to the scriptural accounts we have of this labor. The following facts are established for us in the scriptures:

1. The ability to translate was a gift of God. (D&C 8:4, 6.)

2. The gift of translation was subject to strict obedience, and was withdrawn as a result of disobedience. (D&C 10:1-2.)

3. The Lord also gave the Prophet "power from on high, by the means [Urim and Thummin] which were before prepared, to translate." (D&C 20:8.)

4. In addition to the divine aids granted the Prophet, he was also expected to contribute much to the process through intense study. (D&C 9:1-9.)

5. The spirit of revelation was also necessary to the work of translation. (D&C 8:1-3.)

Joseph Smith's role was appreciably greater than that of amanuensis or scribe. If all the Lord had needed to bring forth the Book of Mormon was a secretary, he could easily have found one more capable than Joseph Smith. Illustrating the importance of that role of the translator, Brigham Young opined that if the Book of Mormon were to be "re-written, in many instances it would materially differ from the present translation." (*JD* 9:311.) No translation of this magnitude, unless dictated directly by God, would be the same, though in principle, content, and spirit it would be identical.

It is also evident that the Lord knew that the first 116 pages translated by Joseph Smith would subsequently be lost by Martin Harris and that they could not be translated again. (1 Nephi 9:5-6; Words of Mormon 1:5-6; D&C 10.) The translation of those 116 pages proved to be a preparatory experience, one granted to allow him to develop his skills as a translator. They served, as it were, as a preparatory school prior to the great work of translation.

As a historical footnote, it is interesting to note that in the work of translation, Joseph Smith discovered that he did not know the English language well. The first edition of the Book of Mormon contained approximately two thousand grammatical errors. When the second edition was printed in 1837 all the grammatical corrections had been made by the Prophet himself.

To the extent that we can reconstruct the work of translation, it appears that it embraces that balance between faith and works we know to be essential to other aspects of the gospel. God would not do for Joseph or Oliver what they, through disciplined effort, could accomplish for themselves, while at the same time he liberally granted divine aid where the task superceded their native abilities.

Joseph's involvement in the translation process demanded that he struggle with the contents of the plates concept by concept, principle by principle, thought by thought, and then give expression to those truths to the satisfaction of the Lord. (D&C 9:9.) Through this process, which demanded complete concentration, he gained an understanding of its doctrines. Thus he obtained both a knowledge and testimony of the "fulness of the gospel" (D&C 20:9) that the Book of Mormon contains.

The work of translation constituted his first comprehensive and systematic study course in gospel principles. It afforded him the opportunity to gain an understanding of basic principles of the gospel that are taught in the Book of Mormon with greater plainness and clarity than in any other scriptural record. Faith, repentance, baptism, receiving the Holy Ghost, enduring to the end, the divine sonship of Christ, the atonement, the gathering of Israel, continuous revelation—all these principles and more were unfolded to him in a manner far superior to that in which they are set forth in the Bible. The continuity of the gospel, that God is the same yesterday, today and forever, that gospel principles are eternal—as are the blessings that flow from them—all would have unfolded to him as he labored with this great scriptural record of the past. The lost 116 pages had provided him the opportunity to gain a proficiency in translation; now his attention could be directed more completely to content, to the substance of the message as he translated.

The doctrines of the Book of Mormon are the foundation upon which the restoration of the gospel rests. They are the principles essential to salvation, and as such, they became the basis of Joseph Smith's gospel understanding through the process of translation.

Defining the spirit of revelation, Joseph Smith said, "A person may profit by noticing the first intimation of the spirit of revelation; for instance, when you feel pure intelligence flowing into you, it may give you sudden strokes of ideas, so that by noticing it, you may find it fulfilled the same day or soon . . . thus by *learning* the Spirit of God and understanding it, you may grow into *the principle of revelation,* until you become perfect in Christ Jesus." (*HC* 3:381. Italics added.) In this statement, Joseph Smith clearly identifies that the Spirit of God is learned and that we grow into the spirit of revelation. Joseph Smith's experiences illustrate that though spiritual gifts are granted by God, they must be developed by man.

In translating the Book of Mormon, the Urim and Thummim were indispensable to the progress of the work. When, because of Martin Harris's defection, the Urim and Thummim were taken from the Prophet for a period, the work of translation ceased. Only after these sacred instruments were returned did the work resume. Even though Joseph Smith had to exert all his mental and spiritual powers to translate, he could not do so at this point in his life without the aid of these seer stones. In addition to the role of the Urim and Thummim in the translation of the Book of Mormon, most of the revelations found in the Doctrine and Covenants that were received prior to the organization of the church were obtained through their aid. Yet the Prophet did not always receive revelations through this means. As he grew in spiritual power, he became less and less dependent on the use of the Urim and Thummim until he had learned and grown in his ability to obtain the mind of the Lord to the extent that he was no longer dependent on external aids. Prior to the organization of the Church and following the completion of the Book of Mormon, the Urim and Thummim were returned to the angel Moroni, and from that point forward, the Prophet received revelation without their help.

That spiritual senses can be developed and strengthened only by use is illustrated in Philo Dibble's account of the manner in which Joseph Smith and Sidney Rigdon received the great revelation on the degrees of glory contained in section 76 of the Doctrine and Covenants. Elder Dibble reports that he and a number of others were present when the revelation was received. He said that he "saw the glory and felt the power, but did not see the vision" itself. He records the conversation that took place between the Prophet and Sidney Rigdon in this language:

"Joseph would, at intervals, say: 'What do I see?' as one might say while looking out of the window and beholding what all in the room could not see. Then he would relate what he had seen or what he was looking at. Then Sidney replied, 'I see the same.' Presently Sidney would say, 'What do I see?' and would repeat what he had seen or was seeing, and Joseph would reply, 'I see the same.'

"This manner of conversation was repeated at short intervals to the end of the vision, and during the whole time not a word was spoken by any other person. Not a sound nor motion made by anyone but Joseph and Sidney, and it seemed to me that they never moved a joint or limb during the time I was there, which I think was over an hour, and to the end of the vision.

"Joseph sat firmly and calmly all the time in the midst of a magnificent glory, but Sidney sat limp and pale, apparently as limber as a rag, observing which, Joseph remarked, smilingly, 'Sidney is not used to it as I am.'" (Hyrum Andrus, *Joseph Smith, the Man and the Seer,* p. 111.)

Shortly after the Church was organized, Joseph Smith was directed to commence a task of such monumental proportions that it remains incomplete even to this day. That task was the translation or revision of the Bible. The nature of this work, which involved both the Old and New Testaments, has been generally misunderstood. Many have supposed that the work consisted of a critical reading and correction of Bible texts based on the Prophet's mastery of the gospel. Such is not the case. The purpose of the labor was, in large measure, a continuation of the systematic schooling of the Prophet in eternal principles that he began when translating the Book of Mormon.

This work of translation involved his poring over Bible texts, laboring to understand their true meanings and to give clarification or make restorations where necessary. The work assumed a degree of ignorance on his part rather than complete understanding. As he sought for understanding and queried of the Lord, answers were given. Simply stated, Joseph Smith was involved in a Bible study program with the Spirit of the Lord as his instructor. The experience is like that which he described when he and Oliver were baptized and filled with the Holy Ghost. Of that occasion he wrote: "Our minds being now enlightened, we began to have the scriptures laid open to our understandings, and the true meaning and intention of their more mysterious passages revealed unto us in a manner which we never could attain to previously, nor ever before had thought of." (JS-H 1:74.)

Many of the important revelations of doctrine available to us today in the Doctrine and Covenants came in response to Joseph Smith's earnest appeal for understanding as he struggled with the meaning of Bible texts. Notable revelations that had this labor as their seedbed include:

Section 45, which deals with the last days and contains explanation and inspired commentary on Matthew 24, wherein the Savior sets forth the signs to precede his second coming.

Section 74, which contains an explanation of 1 Corinthians 7:14.

Section 76, a revelation on the degrees of glory that grew out of Joseph Smith's attempt to understand John 5:29. (D&C 76:15.)

Section 77, a series of questions and answers between Joseph Smith and the Lord on the Book of Revelation.

Section 84, which traces priesthood lineage from Moses back to Adam, and which speaks of the order of things in the Old Testament church and challenges modern priesthood holders to become sons of Moses and Aaron.

Section 86, wherein the Lord explains the parable of the wheat and the tares as it is found in Matthew 13:26-30.

Section 88, which deals primarily with the subject of resurrection, develops concepts that grow out of Paul's discourse on this subject in 1 Corinthians 15.

Section 91, which directs the Prophet not to translate the Apocrypha, even though there is much truth found therein.

Section 93, which quotes from and promises the eventual return of a scriptural record authored by John the Baptist.

Section 107, in which the ancient order of the priesthood is explained, along with a brief account of the meeting at Adam-ondi-Ahman three years previous to Adam's death, and also the promise that in the future we will receive the Book of Enoch.

Section 113, which consists of a series of questions and answers between Joseph Smith and the Lord on Isaiah 11.

Section 132, which was granted in response to Joseph Smith's desire to understand how the Lord justified Old Testament prophets in having a plurality of wives.

There is little question that the greatest benefit that accrued to the Church from Joseph Smith's efforts on the Inspired Version was not the work on the Bible itself, but the understanding he gained from the process and the revelations that we now have that are not only inspired commentary on Bible texts, but are also lucid commentary on eternal principles. This work of translation has been appropriately called the "spiritual education of the Prophet." (Robert J. Matthews, *Joseph Smith's Translation of the Bible,* p. 53.)

Initially, Joseph Smith was not an effective public speaker. Sensing his own limitations in those early years, he relied heavily upon more polished speakers like Oliver Cowdery, Sidney Rigdon, and Parley P. Pratt to do the public preaching. On the day the Church was organized, for instance, the Prophet was content to call upon Oliver Cowdery to deliver this dispensation's first discourse, even though the audience was very small.

Joseph's inability as a public speaker was a matter of prophetic concern. Lehi, repeating a prophecy made by Joseph who was sold into Egypt, likened the latter-day Joseph to Moses. (JST, Genesis 50:29-33; 2 Nephi 3:15, 18.) It will be recalled that Moses was "slow of speech, and of a slow tongue." (Exodus 4:10.) Of him the Lord said, "I will not make him mighty in speaking . . . and I will make a spokesman for him." (2 Nephi 3:17.) In like manner, Lehi said the Lord would grant Joseph Smith a spokesman—a position to which Sidney Rigdon was called by revelation. (D&C 100:9.)

As the years passed and as Joseph's confidence grew, his dependence on Sidney decreased. The transition was completed in 1839 when Joseph, Sidney, and others were in Washington, D.C., presenting their petitions for redress because of the expulsion of the Saints from Missouri. While there they were invited to speak to a group of some three thousand people in one of the largest churches in Philadelphia. Elder Rigdon addressed the congregation first. Fearful of the reaction people might have to pure Mormonism, he defended the restoration with Bible passages, studiously avoiding reference to the coming of angels, visions, and other remarkable spiritual events upon which the restoration rests. According to Parley P. Pratt, Sidney Rigdon's timidity so annoyed Joseph Smith that—

"When he [Sidney Rigdon] was through, brother Joseph arose like a lion about to roar; and being full of the Holy Ghost, spoke in great power, bearing testimony of the visions he had seen, the ministering of angels which he had enjoyed; and how he had found the plates of the Book of Mormon, and translated them by the gift and power of God. He commenced by saying: 'If nobody else had the courage to testify of so glorious a record, he felt to do it in justice to the people, and leave the event with God.'

"The entire congregation were astounded; electrified, as it were, and overwhelmed with the sense of the truth and power by which he spoke, and the wonders which he related. A lasting impression was made; many souls were gathered into the fold. And I bear witness, that he, by his faithful and powerful testimony, cleared his garments of their blood." (*Autobiography of Parley Parker Pratt,* pp. 298-99.)

Thus, Joseph Smith combined his own rugged eloquence with the power of God to become a great orator. Parley P. Pratt described his hard-earned abilities as a speaker in these words:

"His manner was easy and familiar . . . and his language abounding in original eloquence peculiar to himself—not polished—not studied—not smoothed and [polished and] softened by education and refined by art; but flowing forth in its own native simplicity, and profusely abounding in variety of subject and manner. He interested and edified, while, at the same time, he amused and entertained his audience; and none listened to him that were ever weary with his discourse. I have even known him to retain a congregation of willing and anxious listeners for many hours together, in the midst of cold or sunshine, rain or wind, while they were laughing at one moment and weeping the next. Even his most bitter enemies were generally overcome, if he could once get their ears." (Ibid., pp. 45-46.)

By reviewing the experiences of Joseph Smith, we have attempted to find an answer to the question as to when and how the Lord educates his prophets. Our desire has been to discover the extent to which their spiritual education results from personal discipline and effort and to what extent it results from a heavenly endowment. As we review the life of the Prophet, a pattern seems to establish itself. Nothing, we discover, was granted to him without great personal diligence and effort, yet his efforts, no matter how great, were never adequate in and of themselves. He was dependent on divine help. He could not translate the golden plates without combining personal effort with the "gift and power of God." Our answer seems to be found in the balance between these two essential elements.

The same principle seems to find application in his development as a speaker. At first he found himself very dependent on the help of others, but with the passing of years, as he increased in knowledge, understanding, and faith, his abilities as an orator increased also. Again his greatness as a speaker manifested the blending of his personal preparation with the power of God, both elements being absolutely essential. The principle proves consistent as we review the manner in which he gained mastery of gospel principles. We see the Lord taking him through demanding study courses, first in the Book of Mormon and then in the Old and New Testaments and related documents. Line upon line, the gospel was unfolded to him.

Thus we see that great effort was demanded of the Prophet Joseph Smith both before and after his call to prophetic office. His education in the realm of spiritual things was an ongoing process that demanded a balance between his own disciplined efforts and the outpouring of the Spirit of the Lord. If we are to assume that the Lord is consistent in his dealings with the children of men, it becomes a logical assumption that he will demand the same discipline and intensity of effort on our part as he has on the part of his prophets. The course requirements for spiritual excellence remain the same for all students.

THE PROCESS
OF SPIRITUAL GROWTH

*There is no shortcut
to a testimony. (Marion G. Romney.)*

Nothing is imitated more often or counterfeited more frequently than spirituality. The world offers an unlimited variety of vulgarities in the name of religion, ranging from long-faced piety to gross lewdness. Falsehoods have masqueraded as truth and pretense has impersonated genuineness so often that even the discerning can become confused. Nonetheless, toadstools posing as mushrooms in the spiritual realm are as poisonous as their physical counterparts.

Demonstrating their own spiritual callowness, some of the early members of the Church accused Joseph Smith of lacking meekness. He told them that he was "meek and lowly in heart," and that to illustrate the fact, he would personify Christ for a moment. He then proceeded to cry out with a loud voice, "Woe unto you, ye doctors; woe unto you, ye lawyers; woe unto you, ye scribes, Pharisees, and hypocrites!" Then he reminded his reprovers that they could not find the place where he had ever stayed in which he had found fault with the food or complained about the accommodations that were offered him, and suggested that this was what was meant by the meekness and lowliness of Jesus. (*HC* 5:218.)

On another occasion, a couple of pious men of the cloth interrogated the Prophet at length, hoping to find some fault in him. When they stepped out of the house to leave, Joseph drew a line on the ground with his shoe and challenged his visitors to toe the line and see if they could outjump him. They went off in a huff amazed that one who professed to be a man of God would propose such an activity on the Sabbath day. When asked why he had done so, the Prophet responded that they had come to find fault with him, and he hated to see them leave disappointed. (Andrus, *Joseph Smith, the Man and the Seer,* p. 111.)

The efforts of such people to assess true spirituality usually fall as short of the mark as do their efforts to imitate it. To some, spirituality is a sanctimonious list of do's and don'ts; to others it is a religious rally and a bumper sticker. Many are satisfied with a new set of terms to say that what they were doing before is all right. To still others, it is regularity in attending certain religious services or in obeying some other kind of commandment. Some measure spirituality by the zeal with which they vocalize certain tenets and the unrelenting attacks they make on the beliefs of others. For others it takes the form of masochism or personal denial, while there are those who use it as means to hide from the realities of life. Setting all such aside, let us see if by carefully searching the scriptures we can paint a word picture that at least leaves the proper impression in our minds as to what true spirituality is and how it is obtained.

Isaiah declared that "the work of righteousness shall be peace; and the effect of righteousness quietness and assurance forever." (Isaiah 32:17.) Just as it was intended that good works be accomplished quietly, so it is that the attendant spiritual rewards be unobtrusive. God is not a showman, and ostentatious displays quickly alienate his Spirit. Loud and indecorous behaviors provide a sharp contrast with the quiet assurance Isaiah suggested would be characteristic of those whose lives have truly been touched by the Spirit.

One of the most expressive passages dealing with the process of gaining spiritual understanding is found in Doctrine and Covenants 98:12. It reads: "For he will give unto the faithful line upon line, precept upon precept." Then the Lord adds, "and I will try you and prove you herewith." This passage limits the knowledge of spiritual things to the faithful, notes that a process is involved—undoubtedly spanning a significant period of time—and suggests that this slow schooling process of the Lord's will in itself prove to be the test of faith. Faith, like any other spiritual talent, grows gradually and is strengthened as it is used. We will consider the manner in which revelation is granted at greater depth in a subsequent chapter; yet, appropriately it could be noted at this point that the Lord has announced his system for manifesting his will as one in which understanding is granted "line upon line, precept upon precept, here a little and there a little." (2 Nephi 28:30.) Those who are obedient and responsive to this process are rewarded with greater spiritual endowments, while those who announce themselves satisfied with their present state—not desiring to move forward—lose the understanding and light that they once possessed. In both instances, the process is quiet and gradual.

In this same context the Lord has said that those who live gospel principles will "learn wisdom," and then he added, "for unto him that receiveth I will give more; and from them that shall say, We have enough, from them shall be taken away even that which they have." (2 Nephi 28:30.) Two basic concepts are involved here: First, that the key to knowledge is knowledge. That is, obtaining knowledge increases our capacity to obtain still more knowledge. In large measure, we learn by relating things to each other—by identifying how things are similar; thus, the obtaining of knowledge becomes an ever-widening circle.

Conversely, and this is the second concept, when we arrive at the point at which we say "we have enough," we start to lose knowledge. For instance, President Harold B. Lee said of George Washington that he was an educated man because he never went to school—thus he never quit learning. In the realm of spiritual things, any religion that says the heavens are sealed and the Lord no longer speaks begins, like a schoolboy who has closed his books for summer vacation, to forget or lose even that which it had. Even in the realm of spiritual things the rich get richer and the poor get poorer.

Faith comes by righteousness. The Holy Ghost will associate with none but the clean. To the extent to which we are able to sanctify ourselves, we are welcomed into the association of those powers and influences reserved for the pure in heart. "No man is possessor of all things except he be purified and cleansed from all sin. And if ye are purified and cleansed from all sin, ye shall ask whatsoever you will in the name of Jesus and it shall be done." (D&C 50:28-29.) The Lord has said that his eyes are upon us and that he is in our midst though we see him not, "but the day soon cometh that ye shall see me, and know that I am; for the veil of darkness shall soon be rent, and he that is not purified shall not abide the day." (D&C 38:8.)

Nothing in our spiritual growth exceeds in importance the need for good spiritual hygiene. "Let virtue garnish thy thoughts unceasingly," wrote the Prophet; "then shall thy confidence wax strong in the presence of God," and the Holy Ghost become our "constant companion." (D&C 121:45-46.)

If our faith differs from the world, our works will differ also. Since works are produced by faith, if our works are good, our faith is good. The claim to having the same faith as the ancients is evidenced only by producing the same results. If they dreamed dreams, we can dream dreams; if they saw visions, we can see visions; if they entertained angels, we can entertain angels; if they had living prophets and revelation, we too can have living prophets and revelation. If their faith made of them a peculiar people, in like manner we can become a peculiar people.

Works are the roots of faith. A system of beliefs that is not rooted in works of righteousness, like a tree whose branches have outgrown its roots, is vulnerable to uprooting by every wind of doctrine or ideological storm that comes its way. This is why the scriptures teach us that we can know the gospel only to the extent that we live it. Salvation consists in our becoming like God: we do that by learning to think as he thinks, believe as he believes, and do as he would do. (Bruce R. McConkie, *CR*, April 1972, p. 134.)

Having already considered the manner in which Christ advanced from grace to grace, let us now consider the implications of this doctrine as far as men are concerned. Three times within a single sentence we are told that Christ did not receive "a fulness at first," but rather acquired that fulness advancing "from grace to grace." (D&C 93:12-14.) The revelation then proceeds to explain that we have had the process by which Christ obtained perfection taught us in order that we might gain an understanding of how and what to worship, that in due time we too might obtain a fulness of the Father. Salvation, then, consists in our advancing after the manner in which Christ advanced. His salvation did not consist of some divine manifestation of power, nor did it center in some particular event. He worked out his salvation with "fear and trembling" over the course of time by making his works the works of the Father, just as we have been commanded to do.

Christ showed the way; the path that we must walk. Our lot, like his, is to learn the will of the Father and do it, advancing from one grace to another, from good works to greater works, from challenges to greater challenges, from service to greater service, from hope to faith, from faith to power, in all things becoming like unto him. True worship takes the form of works. Thus, in Peter's language we become "partakers of the divine nature" (2 Peter 1:4), or in Joseph Smith's words, we are "assimilated into [his] likeness." (*Lectures on Faith,* p. 66.) Testimony, spiritual strength, salvation itself, become the product of the things we do—not as the world would falsely tell us of some special experience that assures that we will be saved.

God, in his wisdom, grants only that which we are prepared to receive. No purpose would be served by legions of angels coming from the courts on high to preach and teach in our meetings if they spoke a celestial language or taught principles beyond our comprehension. If an angel is going to communicate effectively with a man, he must condescend to speak in the language and according to the understanding of that man. Any other form of communication would be fruitless. Revelation, if it is to be meaningful, cannot exceed that which we are prepared to receive. If our preparation and understanding are puny, then the revelations we receive will be puny. We would not expect God to add to that which we did not improve upon. "Whom shall he teach knowledge, and whom shall he make to understand doctrine?" the scriptures inquire. Answering, we are told, "them that are weaned from the milk, and drawn from the breasts. For precept must be upon precept, precept upon precept; line upon line, line upon line; here a little and there a little." (Isaiah 28:9-10.)

Spiritual growth cannot be programmed. It is not for man to schedule or establish deadlines for the Spirit. The Lord has made it abundantly clear that spiritual blessings are granted according to "his own time, and in his own way, and according to his own will." (D&C 88:68.) The Lord has assured us that if we ask we shall receive, but that the promised blessings will be granted according to his timetable, not ours; confirmation, assurance, understanding, all will come line upon line, precept upon precept, here a little and there a little, as he wills it. "Revelation upon revelation," is the promise, "knowledge upon knowledge, that thou mayest know the mysteries and peaceable things—that which bringeth joy, that which bringeth life eternal. Thou shalt ask, and it shall be revealed unto you in mine own due time. . . ." (D&C 42:61-62.)

We cannot program spiritual growth any more than we can program physical growth. Imagine how silly it would be for a father to call all of his children in and establish goals for each of them as to how much they should grow in the next six months or year, and then to reward or punish them according to their success in meeting the goals he had established. No one questions that proper nourishment, exercise, and rest will facilitate proper growth, but we cannot demand it—we cannot schedule it. As Christ "waited upon the Lord for the time of his ministry to come," so we too must learn patience, doing all we can to facilitate the receipt of such blessings, but not supposing it to be our right to dictate them.

Spiritual growth takes effort. The development of spiritual senses takes time. As we struggle in that process, what we learn today will be so much to our advantage tomorrow. The more we know, the greater our capacity to learn. Gospel principles are not mastered in a few days, weeks, or even months. For us to suppose otherwise is to be like the naive child who assumes his education is complete after a similarly short stint in school. The veil between man and the heavens is not drawn in a day; rather, it is pulled back gradually.

The refining of any of our senses takes time and effort. In that relationship we note with interest that people will commonly compensate for the loss of physical senses by developing others to a more marked degree. The ability to utilize these other senses was always theirs but remained dormant simply because no need required them. Similarly, within the soul of man rests a great host of spiritual senses—these latent spiritual abilities anxiously await a time when we choose to develop them.

REVELATION:
WHEN DO I GET ONE?

*From the time
that Adam first received a communication
from God, to the time that John,
on the Isle of Patmos,
received his communication,
or Joseph Smith had the heavens opened to him,
it always required new revelations,
adapted to the peculiar circumstances
in which the churches
or individuals were placed.
(John Taylor.)*

Y ou can no more be saved by someone else's revelation than you can be saved by their righteousness. Adam's revelation did not tell Noah how to build his ark; Noah's revelation did not tell Lot to forsake Sodom; neither of these instructed Moses as to how he was to free the children of Israel from their Egyptian bondage; and Christ and his disciples were dependent upon none of them. Surely revelation needs to be as constant as the changing circumstances of men. God is the God of the living, not the dead, and he speaks and directs in the affairs of men today with the same ease that he did anciently. Because, as Nephi suggested, he has spoken one word, we need not suppose that he cannot speak another. (2 Nephi 29:9.)

Just as these principles are true of the body of knowledge that constitutes the doctrine of the Church, they are true of the individual testimonies possessed by its members. They too must find their roots, the lifeline of their faith, in personal revelation; for as Joseph Smith taught, there is no salvation without revelation (*HC* 3:389), and it is not a church, but a people that God desires to save.

Though their nation professed to be the true believers, both pious and devout, there were but few of the people in Jesus' day who listened to and believed his words. It was the religious leaders, the Sadducees and Pharisees, who bitterly opposed Christ and his teachings. The Sadducees professed a belief in the Torah (the first five books of Moses), declaring them to be absolute, immutable, and not open to new interpretation. The Pharisees also accepted the Torah, but added to it their belief in the traditions of the fathers. Both effectively rejected the principles of living prophets and continuous revelation. For them the heavens were sealed, revelation had ceased, and they warred with vigor against any who opposed their views. They put Christ to death and sought the lives of his followers. Stephen was stoned to death on the pretense that he rejected Moses—even though his dying testimony was that he accepted Christ because Moses had prophesied of him. (Acts 6:9-15; 7:1-53.)

So it is in our day. The names of the religious sects have changed, but the "war of words and tumult of opinions" remains the same. While the so-called Christian world piously professes allegiance to the Bible, few have actually listened to and believed the book for which they profess such a reverence. The Bible makes no profession to being a comprehensive, exhaustive, or even systematic apology of the gospel—for such it is not! As Paul testified, "Our gospel came not unto you in *word* only, but also in power, and in the Holy Ghost, and in much assurance." (1 Thessalonians 1:5.) All the Bible professes to be is an account of some of God's dealings with some of his children in some of the ages past. The essence of its message is that whenever God has had a people that he acknowledged as his own, he communicated his will to them by revelation, both on a personal basis and through his prophets. Well might those who, like the Sadducees of old, hold to the Bible as absolute and immutable, remind themselves that the experiences that the apostles shared with Christ during the three years of his mortal ministry, and of which we have preserved for us only a fragmentary account, were not sufficient to fully convert them. Their conversion came in large measure from those teachings and sacred experiences they shared with Christ after his resurrection, teachings they felt to be too sacred to preserve for us.

How, then, are we to be converted by a partial account of those experiences which did not convert the apostles?

Chief among those in our day who listened, believed, and responded to the message of the Bible was Joseph Smith. He quickly learned that the "teachers of religion of the different sects understood the same passages of scriptures so differently as to destroy all confidence in settling the question by an appeal to the Bible." While laboring under those difficulties he was directed in his reading to James, first chapter and fifth verse. "If any of you lack wisdom, let him ask of God, that giveth to all men liberally, and upbraideth not; and it shall be given him." "At length," he said, "I came to the conclusion that I must either remain in darkness and confusion, or else I must do as James directs, that is ask God." (JS-H 1:10-13.) Joseph Smith sought God, and, despite the protestations of modern Sadducees and Pharisees, he discovered that the heavens could be opened. True to his promise, God responded to the boy Joseph as he declared he would to all men.

"The voice of the Lord is unto the ends of the earth, that all that will hear may hear." (D&C 1:11.) The promise is that those who have "faith to hear shall hear." (D&C 42:50.) The ability to hear and thus receive is a continuous process. "He that receiveth light," the Lord assured, "and continueth in God, receiveth more light; and that light groweth brighter and brighter until the perfect day." (D&C 50:24.) "For unto him that receiveth I will give more," the Lord announced, "and from them that shall say, We have enough, from them shall be taken away even that which they have." (2 Nephi 28:30.)

The forms of revelation are limitless. Surely it is not for us to place limits or bounds on the heavens specifying when and how God can communicate his will to us. Common forms of revelation include both the spoken and the unspoken word, visitations of angels, dreams, visions, flashes of ideas, impelling impulses, and assurances that come from the Holy Ghost.

Fleeing in the wilderness to escape Jezebel's pledge to kill him, Elijah experienced the varieties of revealed experiences. Sustained by the aid of an angel, he traveled to and lodged himself in a cave at Mount Horeb. There the Lord spoke directly to him, asking, "What doest thou here, Elijah?" Elijah explained his plight and was directed to go "and stand upon the mount before the Lord. And, behold, the Lord passed by, and a great and strong wind rent the mountains, and brake in pieces the rocks before the Lord; but the Lord was not in the wind: and after the wind an earthquake; but the Lord was not in the earthquake: And after the earthquake a fire; but the Lord was not in the fire: and after the fire a still small voice." (1 Kings 19:11-12.)

The hurricane, the earthquake, the lightning were all tokens or manifestations of the power of God, but in none was he disclosed so completely, so convincingly, as in the peaceful calm that followed the tempest, for as he said to Oliver Cowdery, "Did I not speak peace to your mind. . . ? What greater witness can you have. . . ?" (D&C 6:23.)

Even those who have heard the audible voice of the Lord have found it necessary to exert themselves to hear and understand. Recalling the account of the appearance of Christ to the righteous inhabitants of the American continent, we are reminded that the first two times the people heard the voice of his Father who introduced him, they "understood it not." Only the third time the Father spoke did they "open their ears to hear it."

By description we are told that his voice was not harsh, "notwithstanding it being a small voice . . . it did pierce them to the very soul, and did cause their hearts to burn." (3 Nephi 11:3-6.)

Such is the voice one hears as he reads the scriptures under the direction of the Spirit. Joseph Smith's experience as he read the promise of James that God would give to them who asked is a classical illustration of this principle. He said, "Never did any passage of scripture come with more power to the heart of man than this did at this time to mine. It seemed to enter with great force into every feeling of my heart. I reflected on it again and again. . . ." (JS-H 1:12.) All who have read the scriptures with sincerity have, to some degree, experienced such feelings. A thought, an idea, an expression reaches out and burns itself into one's soul. Again and again the thought returns as if an invisible pile driver were hammering it deep within so that in future times it can bear great burdens.

In a revelation given to the twelve apostles the Lord said: "These words are not of men nor of man, but of me; wherefore, you shall testify they are of me and not of man; For it is my voice which speaketh them unto you; for they are given by my Spirit unto you, and by my power you can read them one to another; and save it were by my power you could not have them; Wherefore, you can testify that you have heard my voice, and know my words." (D&C 18:34-36.) Significantly, the Lord told the twelve that they could testify to having heard his voice by reading his words, when they did so under the direction of his Spirit. The revelation was given in 1829, some six years before the appointment of the twelve. Thus we learn that it is not a matter of when a revelation is given, but how it is read that qualifies us to testify we have heard the voice of the Lord. Since there are no principles of salvation that apply to the twelve that do not apply to the members of the Church, all who read under the direction of the Spirit become heirs of this promise.

I have a vivid memory of a missionary meeting at which an apostle stood and said, "The Holy Ghost is present in this meeting." He then instructed each of us to write home and tell our parents that we had been in that presence. Though we felt a great spirit in that meeting, few of us as young missionaries were conscious of the fact that we were actually in the presence of the Holy Ghost. It was helpful to have that formal identification and introduction made. President Harold B. Lee said, "That person is not truly converted until he sees the power of God resting upon the leaders of this Church, and until it goes down into his heart like fire." (CR, April 1972, p. 118.) Too frequently we experience that fire without identifying its source and purpose.

When the report was brought to Moses that two men prophesied in the camp of Israel, one of his young servants spoke up and said, "My lord Moses, forbid them." To this Moses responded, "Enviest thou for my sake? would God that all the Lord's people were prophets, and that the Lord would put his spirit upon them!" (Numbers 11:28-29.) In all dispensations of time it has been the intent of the Lord that the Church of Jesus Christ be a "kingdom of priests" (Exodus 19:6), or, as he said to

Joseph Smith, "that every man might speak in the name of God the Lord, even the Savior of the world. . . ." (D&C 1:20.)

The structure of the Church is such that we are constantly called upon to instruct, inspire, counsel, and bless one another. In doing so, we frequently become the medium for the voice of the Lord. This spiritual interdependency is associated with spiritual gifts; for as the scriptures declare, "all have not every gift given unto them; for there are many gifts, and to every man is given a gift by the Spirit of God. To some is given one, and to some is given another, that all may be profited thereby." (D&C 46:11-12.) There is a great multiplicity of gifts. Some have a marvelous capacity to bear testimony that Jesus is the Christ or that Joseph Smith was a prophet. They do so with greater power and effect than the general membership of the Church and can, by the power of their testimony, lift the spiritual level of a meeting. Others are especially gifted in their ability to teach or preach. All will readily agree that every faithful Latter-day Saint is not an inspiring teacher or necessarily a gifted speaker. While some have the gift of knowledge, others have the gift of wisdom. Such people are constantly sought for help or counsel. Others have the gift of healing, judgment, exhortation, prophecy, the viewing of angels, discerning of spirits, and so on.

These gifts are part of the natural inheritance of the household of faith. They are always found operative among active, faithful members of the Church. Through the use of these gifts we encourage, enlighten, and inspire each other. The operation and manifestation of a gift or gifts in one's life is evidence that the course he is pursuing is approved of the Lord, that his sins have been forgiven, and that the Holy Ghost is associating with him.

God has a personal interest in each of us, but, as President Kimball observed, "it is usually through another person that he meets our needs." (*Ensign,* December 1974, p. 5.) This, he explained, is why it is so important that we be active in the Church, for through our activity we both receive and help others receive direction from the Lord. Whether the direction we need comes from the voice of the Lord himself or from the voice of one of his servants, we have been assured that "it is the same." (D&C 1:38.)

Among the faithful Latter-day Saints, experiences in which they have been able to function beyond their natural abilities are common. Such experiences constitute one of the most prevalent forms of revelation. President Heber J. Grant gives a classical illustration of such an experience. During a meeting in the Salt Lake Tabernacle he noticed his brother, who had been very disinterested and indifferent to the Church, sitting in the audience. Elder Grant bowed his head and silently prayed that if he were requested to speak, he might have the spirit of revelation so that in some manner he might touch the heart of his brother, doing so in a manner that his brother would have to acknowledge to him that he had spoken beyond his natural ability and that he was, in fact, inspired of the Lord. Elder Grant said, "I realized that if he made that confession, then I should be able to point out to him that God has given him a testimony of the divinity of this work."

Elder Grant was invited to speak, which he did with great power. At the conclusion of his remarks, President Angus M. Cannon, who was conducting the meeting, called on George Q. Cannon to occupy the balance of the time. George Q. Cannon said he did not wish to speak. Brother Angus refused to take no for an answer. Finally George Q. Cannon consented and went to the stand and said, in substance:

"There are times when the Lord Almighty inspires some speaker by the revelations of his Spirit, and he is so abundantly blessed by the inspiration of the living God that it is a mistake for anybody else to speak following him, and one of those occasions has been today, and I desire that this meeting be dismissed without further remarks," and he sat down.

Continuing his story Heber J. Grant said, "The next morning my brother came into my office and said, 'Heber, I was at a meeting yesterday and heard you preach,'

"I said, 'The first time you ever heard your brother preach, I guess?'

" 'Oh, no,' he said, 'I have heard you lots of times.'

"I said, 'I never saw you in meeting before.'

" 'No,' he said, 'I generally come in late and go into the gallery. I often go out before the meeting is over. But you never spoke as you did yesterday. You spoke beyond your natural ability. You were inspired of the Lord.' The identical words I had uttered the day before, in my prayer to the Lord. . . .

"I asked, 'What did I preach about yesterday?'

"He replied, 'You know what you preached about.'

"I said, 'Well, you tell me.'

" 'You preached upon the divine mission of the prophet Joseph Smith.'

"I answered, 'And I was inspired beyond my natural ability; and I never spoke before—at any time you have heard me, as I spoke yesterday. Do you expect the Lord to get a club and knock you down? What more testimony do you want of the gospel of Jesus Christ than that a man speaks beyond his natural ability and under the inspiration of God, when he testifies of the divine mission of the Prophet Joseph?' The next Sabbath he applied to me for baptism." (CR, October 1922, pp. 188-90.)

Testimony grows out of consistency in living gospel principles. It is well that we occasionally be reminded that to "just about" live the commandments is to "just about" get the blessings. Our gospel covenants are not suspended by the shining of the sun or the darkness of the night. How grateful we are that God does not abandon his concern for us on holidays, sunny Sundays, and during an annual vacation. But he has warned us that when we are slow to listen to his voice, he will be slow to listen to our prayers—even in the time of our troubles. (D&C 101:7.) Conversely, he has promised that if we will let "virtue garnish" our thoughts "unceasingly," that our confidence will "wax strong" in his presence, the knowledge of heaven will "distil" upon our souls "as the dews from heaven," and the Holy Ghost shall be our constant companion. (D&C 121:45-46.)

Our confidence in the presence of the Lord and the blessings appended to such an association come from living the full gospel law. The promise, for instance, that is given to those who live the Word of Wisdom is limited to those Saints who walk "in obedience to the commandments." (D&C 89:18.) Many in the world have, and do adhere to, strict health laws using great wisdom in that which they eat and drink, but such have not received any promise from the Lord that they will find "wisdom and great treasures of knowledge, even hidden treasures . . . and that the destroying angel shall pass by them. . . ." Such promises are granted only to the Saints who walk in obedience to all the commandments of the Lord. The promise of the Lord is that if we "search diligently, pray always, and be believing," all things will work together for our good if we "walk uprightly" and remember to keep the covenants we have made. (D&C 90:24.) Surely, to such the heavens are and will be open.

REVELATION:
HOW DOES IT COME?

Whom shall he teach knowledge?
and whom shall he make to understand doctrine?
them that are weaned from the milk,
and drawn from the breasts.
For precept must be upon precept,
precept upon precept;
line upon line, line upon line;
here a little, and there a little.
(Isaiah 28:9-10.)

As the dawn precedes the glory of noonday, so the light of heaven quietly chases the darkness of doubt and uncertainty away. Joseph Smith expressed it thus: "As the dews of Carmel, so shall the knowledge of God descend upon them!" (D&C 128:19.) Again and again we are brought back to the premise with which we began that we are involved in a process, not an event. Spirituality is a way of life, not an experience, and it must be found where we live rather than in those places we fondly hope to visit. As with virtually all things of merit, we work to obtain it and realize our efforts only in the course of time. Simply stated, most revelation comes piecemeal, and as the revelations come in bits and pieces, so does our understanding of them. Let us turn to the scriptures for our illustrations.

After the visit of the wise men, an angel of the Lord appeared to Joseph in a dream and directed him to take the young child and Mary and flee into Egypt because Herod sought to kill the child. Joseph's instructions were to remain there until the angel brought him further word. The angel could have instructed them to remain in Egypt for a given length of time and then to return, but he chose not to. Obediently, the holy family left by the dark of night for Egypt, where they remained until Joseph was again visited by an angel. After Herod's death, an angel appeared to Joseph and directed him to "take the young child and his mother, and go into the land of Israel." According to the divine pattern they were to go to Nazareth, but all they were told by the angel was to "go into the land of Israel." Certainly it would have constituted no inconvenience on the part of the angel to give them the additional information, but he did not. It would be unusual for us to direct someone to go to a particular country with no mention being made of a particular city or town, especially if the city or town in which they were to reside was of any importance at all, which in this case it was.

As the holy family returned to the nation of Israel, they learned that Herod's son Archelaus reigned in the place of his father. Joseph and Mary did not feel the child would be safe in the province of Judea. Joseph sought the help of God on the matter and was warned in a dream to continue on to Nazareth of Galilee. (See Matthew 2:13-23.)

The story is remarkably interesting, first, because Mary, the mother of the Christ child, and thus the most honored of all women, a woman capable of dreaming dreams and entertaining angels, was not the recipient of the heavenly manifestations. As marvelous a woman as she was, it was not her stewardship to preside over or protect the family; the angels obviously respected Joseph's province. Second, it is interesting because of the piece-meal manner in which Joseph's instructions came. It was as though the Lord were saying to him "Proceed in faith, prove yourself, and when additional instructions are necessary I will give them to you."

We have reason to believe that Lehi was an experienced traveler, probably a merchant by profession. When the Lord directed him to take his family and flee Jerusalem, he had no difficulty determining what provisions would be needed, and it appears that he had the necessary tents and other equipment in his possession. (1 Nephi 2:2.) Though we have but an abbreviated account of his wilderness journey, the evidence is that he planned well and that he and his family were adequately prepared. We note with interest that it was only after they had journeyed into the wilderness that the Lord spoke again and directed that Lehi's sons return to Jerusalem and obtain the plates of brass from Laban. (1 Nephi 3:2-3.) Now the Lord knew, even if Lehi did not, that it would be vitally important for Lehi's family to have those records, and He knew it before they left Jerusalem. This raises the question as to why they did not make some kind of arrangement for the plates before they left, thus avoiding the need for the return trip.

Shortly after Lehi's sons successfully returned with the plates, the Lord spake again unto him, this time directing him to have the boys return once again to Jerusalem to persuade Ishmael and his family of daughters to join them, thus providing women for his sons to marry. Again the question is raised as to why this matter was not attended to either before they initially left Jerusalem or when the boys returned for the plates. If it had not occurred to Lehi that his sons would need wives, surely it would have occurred to Sariah or one of the sons. (1 Nephi 7:1-2.)

Since we have the assurance that the Lord's house is a house of order, we can only conclude that there is reason and purpose in the order and timing of these revelations. They resulted in great lessons being learned and obviously provided Laman, Lemuel, Sam, and Nephi with the opportunity to show what they were made of. We recall Nephi's splendid statement of his plan of attack as he went to obtain the plates: "I was led by the Spirit, not knowing beforehand the things which I should do." (1 Nephi 4:6.)

Our prophets are constantly seeking divine direction in the choosing of those who will be our leaders in the Church. The traditional pattern for their selection was established anciently. Consider by way of illustration the manner in which David was chosen to be Saul's successor in Israel. The prophet Samuel, grieved at Saul's rebellion, implored the Lord as to what should be done and was directed to fill his horn with oil and go to the house of Jesse the Bethlehemite, for the Lord said, "I have provided me a king among his sons."

Translating this story into a modern setting, we could liken it to one of the Brethren being sent out to reorganize a stake, though in this instance Samuel had one tactical problem that they would not have today—namely, Saul. Samuel assumed that if Saul learned what he was doing, he would be killed. Counseling with the Lord on the matter, he was instructed to take a heifer with him and indicate that he was going to Bethlehem to offer a sacrifice. Once there he was to invite Jesse to the sacrifice; then, the Lord said, "I will shew thee what thou shalt do: and thou shalt anoint unto me him whom I name unto thee."

There was no question in the Lord's mind as to who was to be the new king of Israel, but he obviously had no intention of telling Samuel about it in advance of his doing as he had been instructed.

Continuing our analogy, the General Authority sent to reorganize a stake goes without any predetermination as to who will be called to lead—in fact, in most instances, as was the case with Samuel, he finds himself calling someone he had not known previously.

After offering his sacrifice, Samuel instructed Jesse to have each of his sons pass before him. Eliab, Jesse's oldest son, came forward and Samuel was immediately impressed with his stature and appearance. He looked like a leader. Confirmation of the choice was sought from the Lord, but was refused. Thus Samuel was reminded that the Lord's concern was not with the outward appearance of a man, but with his heart. Seven more of Jesse's sons passed before Samuel and still none were chosen.

Samuel then inquired of Jesse, "Are here all thy children?" Jesse confessed that there was still another, one for whom perhaps they were a little embarrassed and whom they had sent off to tend the sheep. Samuel insisted that he be brought. When David arrived the Lord spoke and said, "Arise, anoint him: for this is he." (See 1 Samuel 16:1-12.)

As we review this story, it is evident that the Lord could easily have said to Samuel in the first place, "Go down to Bethlehem to the house of Jesse and ordain his youngest son David to be my king," but such was not the manner of the Lord anciently any more than it is today. He does not reveal to his servants today who should preside over a stake before they go to that stake, interview its leaders, seek their recommendation, make a decision, and then seek a spiritual confirmation of that decision.

As the pattern of divine direction unfolds, it appears to be commonly accompanied by tests of obedience and faith along with the teaching of great lessons.

Victory was assured to the army of Israel in their battles with the heathen inhabitants of Canaan as long as they kept their covenants with exactness. A cardinal command was that none of the spoils of war be taken, emphasizing that the victory belonged to God alone. When they suffered a humiliating defeat in their battle with the city-state of Ai, a distraught Joshua rent his clothes, prostrated himself before the ark of the covenant, and beseeched the Lord for an explanation. "Alas, O Lord God," he cried, "wherefore hast thou at all brought this people over Jordan, to deliver us into the hand of the Amorites, to destroy us? would to God we had been content, and dwelt on the other side Jordan! O Lord, what shall I say, when Israel turneth their backs before their enemies! For the Canaanites and all the inhabitants of the land shall hear of it, and shall environ us round, and cut off our name from the earth: and what wilt thou do unto thy great name?

"And the Lord said unto Joshua, Get thee up. . . . Israel hath sinned, and they have also transgressed my covenant which I commanded them: for they have even taken of the accursed thing, and have also stolen, and dissembled also, and they have put it even among their own stuff. Therefore the children of Israel could not stand before their enemies, but turned their backs before their enemies, because they were accursed: neither will I be with you any more, except ye destroy the accursed from among you."

Joshua was instructed that in the morning each of the twelve tribes was to be marched before him in order that it might be manifested to him among which tribe the covenant breaker was a part. That tribe was then to be marched before him according to families so that the family of the culprit might be identified. Following this, the culprit's family was to be marched before him according to households so that the household might be identified. And finally, the household was to be marched before him man by man so that the transgressor might be found.

The process was a dramatic one; it involved all of Israel— every man, woman, and child—and undoubtedly consumed a number of hours before the man Achan was identified. Achan was invited to confess, which he did. His hidden treasures were surrendered, while all Israel witnessed his shame. According to the directive of the Lord, Achan, his family, and all that he had were destroyed. (See Joshua 7.)

As we reflect upon this story, we realize that it would have been a simple matter for the Lord to reveal Achan's perfidy to Joshua even before his troops were defeated at Ai, and certainly he could have done so without the necessity of having all Israel parade before the prophet. In doing so, however, a great teaching moment would have been lost and a dramatic lesson for all of Israel forfeited. Joshua, who had sufficient faith and power in his priesthood to part the waters of the Jordan so all Israel could pass over on dry ground, and who could command the sun and the moon to stand still and have them obey his command, also found it necessary to struggle with the things of the spirit and to gain his knowledge of the mind of the Lord "line upon line."

Perhaps no conversion to the gospel has been more dramatic than Paul's. A proud and strict Pharisee, he became an ardent persecutor of the Christians. While on the road to Damascus, where he sought the followers of Christ with the intent of bringing them bound to Jerusalem, he saw a light and heard a voice from the heavens. From the midst of the light he heard that voice saying, "Saul, Saul, why persecutest thou me?" Trembling, Paul (then Saul) asked, "Lord, what wilt thou have me to do?" He was instructed to go into the city of Damascus, where he would learn the will of the Lord concerning himself. Again we see the scriptural pattern begin to unfold. Full and complete instructions are not given, but merely the direction: Go into the city and you will be told.

Blinded by the vision, he had to be led by his companions into the city. There he sat in darkness for three days, neither eating nor drinking, but laboring in prayer as he sought to correct the course of his life and to receive the instruction promised by the Lord. The Lord directed Ananias, the local leader of the church, and undoubtedly one of those on the list whom Paul had sought to arrest, to go to Paul, heal him of his blindness, preach the basic principles of the gospel to him, and then baptize him and give him the gift of the Holy Ghost. Paul then spent "certain days" with the disciples at Damascus being schooled in the principles of the kingdom preparatory to the great ministry that would be his. (See Acts 9:3-19.)

As miraculous as Paul's experience was on the Damascus road when he saw the light and heard the voice of the Lord, it did not grant him a remission of sins; it did not give him the companionship of the Holy Ghost or a knowledge of the saving principles of the gospel; nor did it grant him a call to serve in the church and kingdom of God. All of these blessings were to come, but when they came, they came under the hands of his priesthood leaders. Paul had a marvelous experience that placed him on the path, the pursuit of which would eventually lead him to great knowledge and power with God and ultimately to eternal life. But Paul, like all men, had to pursue that path step by step, learning first the great importance of his priesthood leaders as the source of the answer to his question, "What wilt thou have me to do?"

A companion story to that of the conversion of Paul is the baptism of Cornelius, the gentile centurion. Cornelius is described as being a devout and God-fearing man. He gave freely to the poor and was respected as being just among the Jews— something that certainly was not said of many Roman soldiers. He presided over his household in righteousness and prayed continually. One afternoon while he was praying, an angel from God appeared to him and, addressing him by name, said, "Thy prayers and thine alms are come up for a memorial before God. And now send men to Joppa and call for one Simon, whose surname is Peter: . . . he shall tell thee what thou oughtest to do." (See Acts 10:1-6.)

Cornelius was being directed to seek the answers to his questions as to what he ought to do from the man whom the Lord had called to stand at the head of his church and be his mouthpiece to all the world in that age. The thread that binds all our stories together becomes more evident. Surely the Lord was capable of answering Cornelius's questions, as was the angel who came as a messenger to him, but such is not the pattern and manner of the Lord. He had established his kingdom and appointed his mouthpiece. His purpose was not to give Cornelius some kind of experience that would make him independent of the prophet or the church. Rather, it was to lead him to it; hence the directive to give a listening ear to his earthly spokesman, for "he shall tell thee what thou oughtest to do."

In this experience of Cornelius is found the rod by which all so-called spiritual experiences claimed by those outside the church and kingdom of God can be measured. The test is simply to ask, What is its purpose? If its purpose is to encourage the recipient to give a listening ear to the Lord's prophet, to "seek counsel, and authority, and blessings constantly" from under his hand, it comes from God. Conversely, if its purpose is to place one in a position wherein he rejects the Lord's prophets, claiming he has been saved by being the recipient of some supernatural experience, it does not come from God.

To conclude our story, Cornelius sent for Peter and Peter came. Cornelius gathered his family and friends around him and bade them listen to Peter's message. The Spirit was manifest in great abundance. "The Holy Ghost fell on all them which heard the word," and they spoke in tongues, went forth at Peter's direction, and were baptized. (See Acts 10:44-48.)

From our scriptural case studies we learn that revelation is preceded by work, faith, obedience, and proper purpose. We learn that it comes through the appointed channels or sources, and that the Lord has never granted a promise to save anyone independent of those channels. We learn that he has great respect for his priesthood leaders and expects us to do likewise. They constitute the basic source to which we are to turn to know the course we ought to pursue.

We have seen that revelation comes most frequently in a piecemeal fashion and that, like all knowledge, it is granted according to our preparation. We learn in relation to what we know. The more we know, the greater our capacity to learn. Thus we see the Master Teacher revealing or rationing the light of heaven according to our spiritual levels of maturation. For the most part the process is quiet, natural, and gradual. Answers come as we are ready for them. Principles are taught "line upon line" that we might embrace them. Precepts are added to precepts, and our faith is rewarded "here a little and there a little."

ASKING QUESTIONS
AND GETTING ANSWERS

Ask the Father in my name,
in faith believing that you shall receive,
and you shall have the Holy Ghost,
which manifesteth all things which are
expedient unto the children of men.
(D&C 18:18.)

The living God is a speaking God. There is no scriptural promise repeated more frequently than the assurance that we can ask of God and receive answers. In this marvelous promise, which affirms the principle of continuous revelation, we do not anticipate nor do we find a suspension of any gospel principles. The promise of spiritual riches has never been given indiscriminately. This promise, for instance, does not release us from the responsibility to study, pray, and obey. When Laman and Lemuel declared that the Lord did not make things known unto them, Nephi called their attention to their own scriptural records, asking, "Do ye not remember the things which the Lord hath said?—If ye will not harden your hearts, and ask me in faith, believing that ye shall receive, with diligence in keeping my commandments, surely these things shall be made known unto you." (1 Nephi 15:11.) Because there was no diligence upon the part of Laman and Lemuel in keeping the commandments, the promise could not be realized.

So it was from the beginning. God taught his principle to Adam in these words: "If thou wilt turn unto me, and hearken unto my voice, and believe, and repent of all thy transgressions, and be baptized, even in water, in the name of mine Only Begotten Son, who is full of grace and truth, which is Jesus Christ, the only name which shall be given under heaven, whereby salvation shall come unto the children of men, ye shall receive the gift of the Holy Ghost, asking all things in his name, and whatsoever ye shall ask, it shall be given you." (Moses 6:52.)

Faith, repentance, baptism, and receipt of the Holy Ghost have been the requisites of this promise in all generations of men. Those who hunger and thirst after righteousness have been promised that they will be filled. From the Inspired Version of the Bible, we learn that it is the Holy Ghost with which they will be filled. (JST, Matthew 5:8.) From this source we also learn that the promises in the Beatitudes were not made to the multitudes; rather, they were made to the apostles, who were told, "blessed are they who shall believe on your words, and come down into the depth of humility, and be baptized in my name; for they shall be visited with fire and the Holy Ghost, and shall receive a remission of their sins." (JST, Matthew 5:4.) It was in the context of this doctrine that the disciples were sent forth to teach others to "ask of God" with the appended hope that they too might receive as they complied with the same eternal principles. (JST, Matthew 7:1, 12.)

The true spirit of prayer is one in which we seek the will of God in preference to personal desires. As revealed to Joseph Smith, the principle was stated: "He that asketh in the Spirit asketh according to the will of God; wherefore it is done even as he asketh." (D&C 46:30.) And again, "know this, it shall be given you what you shall ask. . . ." (D&C 50:30.) To these statements we could add the testimony of John the Beloved, who wrote, "And this is the confidence that we have in him, that, if we ask anything according to his will, he heareth us." (1 John 5:14.)

The key to receiving answers to prayer is in asking the right questions. The Lord does not permit the desires and faith of righteous and devout men to override his purposes. The Savior himself pleaded, "Abba, Father, all things are possible unto thee; take away this cup from me." Yet lest he pray for that which he should not, he hastened to add, "nevertheless, not my will, but thine be done." (JST, Mark 14:40.) It is an eternal principle that we cannot "exercise faith contrary to the plan of heaven." (HC 2:15.)

Joseph Smith recorded for us an occasion on which he apparently prayed for knowledge that was beyond his right to know. "I was once praying very earnestly," he said, "to know the time of the coming of the Son of Man, when I heard a voice repeat the following: 'Joseph, my son, if thou livest until thou art eighty-five years old, thou shalt see the face of the Son of Man; therefore let this suffice, and trouble me no more on this matter.' " The Prophet said he did not have any idea whether this had reference to the beginning of the millennium, an appearance of Christ previous to the millennium, or an opportunity he would have to see the face of Christ after he had died and left this mortal existence. (D&C 130:14-16.) Even though Joseph held the keys of all spiritual blessings and the right to have the mysteries of the heavens opened to him, he could not obtain an answer to this question. (D&C 107:18-19.) What he did receive, however, was this promise and counsel as to what we should pray for: "Whatsoever ye ask the Father in my name it shall be given unto you, *that is expedient for you;* And if ye ask anything that is not expedient for you, it shall turn unto your condemnation." (D&C 88:64-65. Italics added.)

Teaching this principle to the Nephite nation, Christ said: ". . . whatsoever ye shall ask the Father in my name, which is right, believing that ye shall receive, behold it shall be given unto you." (3 Nephi 18:20.) In like manner, Nephi, who successfully sought to "see, and hear, and know" the great things that had been manifested to his father, testified of a God who would give liberally if one asked "not amiss." (1 Nephi 10:17; 2 Nephi 4:35.) James explained that some would ask in vain because their intent was wrong. (James 4:3.) From the writings of the prophets it becomes plain that the heavens will not be parted to satisfy idle curiosity.

Near a major freeway a towering neon sign announces "Christ Is the Answer." As I have passed that sign I have found myself asking, "But what is the question?" Right questions precede right answers. Prayers are answered for those with the wisdom and inspiration to ask the right questions, questions that conform to the will of God and the laws of heaven. "If ye abide in me, and my words abide in you," Christ said, "ye shall ask what ye will, and it shall be done unto you." (John 15:7.)

In an interview with Brigham Young, the diminutive Tom

Thumb is said to have indicated there were some things he could not understand about Mormonism. Brigham Young reportedly responded: "Don't worry, when I was your size I didn't understand [them] either. (Nels Anderson, *Desert Saints,* p. 390.)

It takes spiritual stature to see and understand much that is in the realm of the Spirit. John Taylor said our minds need to be continually "on the stretch after the things of God." (*JD* 1:368.) We stretch our minds by living the gospel; thus, as our understanding grows, our righteousness grows. It is through this process that we learn to ask the right questions and obtain the attendant promise that we will receive answers.

Study and prayer are the parents of revelation. To those who ponder the things of the Spirit the Lord has said: "I will tell you in your mind and in your heart, by the Holy Ghost, which shall come upon you and which shall dwell in your heart." He added that this was the "spirit of revelation." (D&C 8:2-3.) Among the greatest spiritual manifestations given to men are Nephi's experience on the high mountain, Joseph Smith's vision of the degrees of glory, and Joseph F. Smith's vision of the redemption of the dead. Each of these manifestations grew out of a situation in which the man involved was pondering or meditating on the teachings of the prophets. (See 1 Nephi 10:17-22; 11:1; D&C 76:19; JFS—V.) It is through the process of pondering or meditating that most revelations come.

To ponder or meditate is to think deeply. It involves a union of mind and spirit in a form of study and prayer. It is the process by which we labor to induce the Spirit to guide our study so we might find the treasures of the Spirit and gain understanding, for real gospel understanding can be gained in no other way. It was not enough for the Nephite nation to have the resurrected Christ as their teacher. At the conclusion of a day's teaching, he directed them to return to their homes where they could ponder what he had taught them and ask the Father, in his name, for understanding. Only in this manner could they prepare themselves to receive further teachings at his hand. (3 Nephi 17:3.) It is one thing to have a vision and another to understand that vision. Nephi said, "My heart pondereth continually upon the things which I have seen and heard." (2

Nephi 4:16.) Only through such a process can we obtain the understanding we seek.

Moroni's counsel to those who desired to know the truthfulness of the Book of Mormon is that they first ponder its message. It is in such a process, Moroni tells us, that we can seek to know of its truthfulness. (Moroni 10:3-5.) As we ponder the Book of Mormon, we are confronted with numerous internal evidences of its truthfulness. Foremost among these are the doctrines it teaches. The Book of Mormon has no scriptural peer in teaching the doctrines of the fall, the atonement, and the need for a Redeemer. The clarity with which it testifies that Jesus is the Christ is unmatched in any other scriptural record. Nor is there a scriptural record that is its equal in exposing the enemies of Christ and confounding false doctrines. Again and again, as we read this sacred volume and ponder its great message, we are left to ask, Could Joseph Smith have written this? Repeatedly the Spirit affiirms that this is not the work of a man.

If we were to delete every revelation in the Doctrine and Covenants that came to Joseph Smith in response to his questions, we would have relatively few verses remaining. What a marvelous thing it is that Joseph Smith took the instruction to "ask" literally. The implication is that even those worthy to receive revelation have not always received it simply because they did not desire it. Christ told his disciples in the old world that he had other followers, not of their number, whom he would visit. (John 10:16.) Since they made no inquiries about the matter, he volunteered no further information. While visiting the Nephites, he explained that they were the ones to whom he had reference in making the statement to his Old World disciples. He told these New World followers there were still others whom he would visit, having reference specifically to the lost tribes. He instructed the Nephites to record that information in order that there be a record, in case those in Jerusalem never asked about the matter. (3 Nephi 16:4.)

The scriptures identify a reluctance to pray as a symptom of spiritual illness. Diagnosing the source of such feelings, Nephi declared, "The evil spirit teacheth not a man to pray, but teacheth him that he must not pray." (2 Nephi 32:8.) Brigham Young's prescription for such an ailment was prayer. Pray until you feel like praying, was his counsel. A voracious spiritual appetite evidences good spiritual health. To be spiritually healthy is to hunger and thirst after the things of the Spirit.

The Spirit of the Lord does not fear truth. Such a Spirit does not teach men to shun prayer or avoid spiritual investigation in any form. "Prove all things," the apostle Paul directed, and "hold fast that which is good." (1 Thessalonians 5:21.) It is a simple matter to identify the source of promptings among those who reject the message of the restoration without having heard it. Yet such experiences are common among those who do missionary work. For instance, one of my students reported that her family gave a friend a copy of the Book of Mormon with the challenge to read it. The friend immediately went out and purchased an anti-Mormon book, which he read instead, and then decided upon that evidence that the Book of Mormon could not be true. As is the case with most Book of Mormon critics, it was not necessary for him to have read it to reject it. If this same friend had been given a copy of the New Testament, would he have gone in search of a book written by Caiaphas or another of the Sanhedrin that condemned Christ to death? Would he reject Christ and his teachings on the testimony of his enemies? Surely that is what he is doing in rejecting the Book of Mormon.

Had those who rejected and opposed Christ prayerfully considered his message? Would that have been necessary when they knew that the unlearned Galilean consorted with publicans and sinners? Was it not common knowledge that he was both "gluttonous, and a winebibber?" (Matthew 11:19.)

The Lord said that those that sought to confound Joseph Smith did so "because their deeds [were] evil; therefore," he said, "they will not ask of me." (D&C 10:21.) That spirit which sustains a man in refusing to listen and refusing to pray is the same spirit that has opposed Christ and his prophets in all ages past.

Three years after the death of Joseph Smith, Brigham Young saw and conversed with him in a dream. Instructing President Young as to how the Saints were to know and identify the Spirit of the Lord, Joseph said that it would "whisper peace and joy to their souls," take malice, hatred, strife, and evil in all its forms from their hearts, and leave them with the desire to do right and to labor to bring forth the kingdom of God. (As told by Marion G. Romney, *Conference Report,* April 1944, pp. 140-41.) Even before the organization of the Church, the Lord told Hyrum Smith to "trust in that Spirit which leadeth to do good—yea, to do justly, to walk humbly, to judge righteously," for, the Lord said, "this is my Spirit." Association with this Spirit, Hyrum was assured, would enlighten his mind, bring him joy, and enable him to know all things pertaining to righteousness. (D&C 11:12-14.)

Elder Boyd K. Packer remarks that he once heard Marion G. Romney say, "I always know when I am speaking under the inspiration of the Holy Ghost because I always learn something from what I've said." (*Teach Ye Diligently,* p. 304.) This is also an appropriate standard for identifying the presence of the Spirit of the Lord in our personal study and reflection. The Holy Ghost is a teacher, and our association with him is always one in which we learn, are challenged, feel inspired, and are uplifted.

WHEN NO SURE
ANSWER COMES

Take, my brethren,
the prophets, who have spoken
in the name of the Lord,
for an example of suffering, affliction,
and of patience.
(James 5:10.)

Not infrequently important decisions for which we seek spiritual direction are associated with deadlines. We ask: What do we do when a deadline has arrived and we have been unable to identify a sure course, or we lack the spiritual confirmation that we seek? On the heels of such questions comes the soul searching as to why we have been unable to obtain answers, with the attendant apprehension about personal worthiness and wondering as to why the Lord has forgotten us.

Let us consider some possible responses to these questions. In doing so we will assume that we have lived so as to have claim to inspiration; that is, that we are living right and have to the best of our understanding done the things the Lord would expect of us in order to receive divine direction. This would include having studied the matter out in our mind, made a decision, and sought spiritual confirmation for that decision. Yet despite our efforts, the assurance we desire has not come and the deadline for the decision has arrived.

Since even indecision would impose a decision on us, if we are going to remain agents unto ourselves, we are obligated to consciously choose the course we will follow. We choose that course with the realization that we are at the same time choosing to live with the consequences of that decision. Our obligation then is to exercise the best judgment we can and make a decision. We make such decisions with the appended faith that if they are acceptable to the Lord he will bless our course, and that in due time the confirmation we seek will come. On the other hand, if the course we have chosen is not appropriate in the eyes of the Lord, and since we are still seeking his will, our faith is that he will intervene and prevent any circumstances that would not ultimately be in our best interest.

Still the question persists as to why we were unable to get an answer and save ourselves such anguish and difficulties. To this we can only respond that life is a schoolmaster with some hard lessons to teach, and it is not in the providence of the Lord that people of faith be excused from life's difficult courses. It is almost axiomatic that life's greatest lessons come out of its greatest struggles. In the twilight years of his life, Elder Hugh B. Brown observed that he had "learned more from brick bats than bouquets." Faith, wisdom, judgment, all have their roots in such experiences. As the child must learn to stand on his own and then to walk without assistance, so we too must learn to stand alone and walk alone as we meet some of life's difficult challenges.

The Lord told Joseph Smith, "A man may receive the Holy Ghost, and it may descend upon him and not tarry with him." (D&C 130:23.) The implication of this passage is not that un-worthiness has forced the Holy Ghost to flee, but rather that there are those occasions in which the Lord leaves us to our own devices and understanding. Elder Bruce R. McConkie has explained that "even a righteous person is often left to himself so that he does not at all times enjoy the promptings of revela-tion and light from the Holy Ghost." (*Mormon Doctrine*, p. 313.) "The Holy Ghost in person may visit men," explained President Joseph F. Smith, "and will visit those who are worthy and bear witness to their spirit of God and Christ, but not tarry with them." Such visits he said would come "from time to time." (*Gospel Doctrine*, p. 61.)

The promise of the Lord is that those of his servants who are sufficiently humble will be "blessed from on high, and re-ceive knowledge from time to time." (D&C 1:28.) There must of necessity be those times when answers will not come and we must utilize our own best judgment trusting in the overriding hand of providence.

While the Church was yet in its infancy, the Lord let it be known that it was not appropriate that we be directed by him in all the affairs of our lives. (D&C 58:26.) Such a course would result in the loss of agency and the forfeiture of stewardships, and would deprive us of the opportunity to grow in wisdom and understanding. The directive of the Lord was that we apply ourselves with all diligence to the various affairs of life without waiting for revelation concerning every duty or decision, but to constantly counsel with him. (D&C 58:25.) Within the bounds of righteousness we frequently find great latitude for choice. Those choices made with spiritual-mindedness, will be approved and blessed by the Lord. Thus Nephi counseled that we do not "perform anything unto the Lord" without first asking the Father in the name of Christ to consecrate that performance to the end that it will work toward the welfare of our souls. (2 Nephi 32:9.)

"It is a great thing to inquire at the hands of God, or to come into His presence," counseled Joseph Smith, "and we feel fearful to approach him on subjects that are of little or no consequence. . . ." (HC 1:339.) From a series of revelations in the Doctrine and Covenants, we learn that the early missionaries of this dispensation had a tendency to inquire of the Lord concerning matters that should have been decided on the basis of their own judgment.

In 1831 the Lord directed certain elders to accompany Joseph Smith as he returned from Jackson County, Missouri, to Kirtland, Ohio. Faced with a decision as to how they should travel, they had the Prophet inquire of the Lord as to whether they should buy a craft or make one. The response of the Lord was "It mattereth not unto me." (D&C 60:5.) As these elders traveled down the Missouri River they experienced a number of dangers, so they again had the Prophet inquire of the Lord as to whether they should continue to travel on the water or if it would be better for them to travel by land. Again the response of the Lord was "It mattereth not unto me," and directed them to make it a matter of their own judgment. (D&C 61:22.) As they continued their journey they met several elders who were on their way to Jackson County. By revelation the Prophet directed them to complete their mission to Jackson and then to return to the East. Returning to Ohio, they were invited to travel as a group or by twos, whichever seemed most appropriate. For the Lord said, "It mattereth not unto me; only be faithful," to your mission of declaring the gospel. (D&C 62:5.)

Obviously the faith and zeal with which these brethren proceeded on their appointed missions and the manner in which they declared the gospel was of great concern to the Lord. Their mode of travel and many decisions en route were to be left to their own prayerful judgment. Perhaps this principle is best illustrated with the call of Stephen Burnett to serve as a missionary. The commandment of the Lord to him was that he go into the world and preach "whether to the north or to the south, to the east or to the west," the Lord said, "it mattereth not, for ye cannot go amiss." (D&C 80.) This revelation then proceeded to give specific instructions as to what and how Elder Burnett was to teach.

Apparently it made no difference to the Lord where Elder Burnett labored as long as he labored. As is so often the case, it was not a matter of where he served, but rather how he served. Frequently that is the case with all of us. The Lord has a greater concern with how we labor than where we labor, with what we do than with where we do it.

Joseph Smith taught that we do not inquire at the hand of God for revelation unless there is none existent that addresses the need. (HC 1:339.) Once the Word of Wisdom, the law of tithing, or any gospel principle has been revealed, there is no need for the Lord to give them anew to each succeeding prophet or generation. A classical illustration of this principle is the order of succession in the presidency of the Church. Illustrating this order, Elder Bruce R. McConkie explained that at the death of Harold B. Lee no revelation was needed for Council of the Twelve to know what the mind and will of the Lord was. It was by then an established principle that the senior apostle be the mouthpiece of the Lord. Elder McConkie said: "It was not required, nor was it requisite or needed, that the Lord give any revelation, that any special direction be given. The law was already ordained and established. God does not look down each morning and say, 'The sun shall rise.' He has already established the law, he has set the sun in the firmament, and the sun operates in harmony with established law in its rising. And so it was with the transfer of leadership from President Lee to President Kimball." (*BYU Speeches of the Year,* January 8, 1974.)

We have no claim to revelation on matters that have already been plainly revealed. When we seek such, we become something like the young boy who sought to excuse his lateness to dinner with the announcement that he did not hear the first two times he was called. Before we seek new revelations, Brigham Young suggested that we ought to live up to what we have. (*JD* 6:319.)

There is no better evidence of spiritual maturity than that of patience. As James counseled anciently: "Let patience have her perfect work, that ye may be perfect and entire, wanting nothing." (James 1:4.) Patience has always been an attribute of men of faith. In some instances, the confirmation we seek has not come because we have not completed the sifting or studying process necessary. In others, it may be that we seek counsel on matters that we ought to determine for ourselves. And in still other cases, the development of the attributes of Godliness may exceed in importance our receiving immediate answers and directions. Thus there will be those occasions when it is necessary for us to proceed with the best judgment we can make, for it will only be in the application of that decision that the answer we seek will be made plain. Though we may feel anguish and frustration, the promise is still ours, "that all these things shall give [us] experience, and shall be for [our] good." (D&C 122:7.)

CHARACTERISTICS
OF A VALID TESTIMONY

*Competence as a witness
is predicated upon knowledge.*
(Henry D. Moyle.)

Imagine yourself dragged into a court of law and accused of a heinous crime. Suppose also that the attorneys for the prosecution in presenting their case against you produced no evidence. Instead they called person after person to the witness stand to testify that they "believed" you were guilty. Given the chance, you would argue that it would be a strange system of justice that allowed a man to be convicted of a crime simply because his accusers "believed" him to be guilty or because he had the misfortune to look like a criminal. The illustration helps bring into focus the fact that because someone believes something does not in itself make him a competent witness whose testimony should be given credence.

Orson Pratt declared that "a person cannot be a witness to that which he merely believes." (*JD* 16:209.) Suppose, for instance, that you testified that Jesus was the Christ, using as your evidence the fact that you had carefully studied the Bible, which declared that to be the case. Certainly someone else should be equally entitled to testify that Jesus was not the Christ basing their argument on the fact that they too had diligently studied the Bible and, having done so, were quite convinced that Christ was not the promised Messiah. You and your antagonist could argue the matter at length, but when the dust finally settles it will cover you both. Neither conviction nor understanding grows out of such a process.

In like manner, suppose some renowned scientist takes up the cause, declaring that no one can deny the existence of God because of the multitude of evidences in nature, and then commences to substantiate his testimony with illustration after illustration. Would not another scientist be entitled to present his list of contradictions to all the arguments of the first scientist? Could he not, with some justification, as many have, declare "We have the same evidence as you and from that evidence we have drawn different conclusions"?

The problem in both instances is that the participants are substituting belief for knowledge. Because they cannot speak of that which they have seen, heard, or personally experienced, their testimony is without value. Most discussions of spiritual things center around the kind of evidence that courts of law regard as hearsay—the participants are simply not competent witnesses. Elder LeGrand Richards illustrates this with the following experience:

"A few years ago a group of ministers were passing through Salt Lake en route to Los Angeles to attend a ministerial convention. They stopped over in Salt Lake City. They wanted to ask some questions about our teachings, and arrangements were made for them to meet one of the Twelve in the conference room in the Church Office Building. After that member had answered their questions, he bore his solemn witness that he knew that Jesus was the Christ, that Joseph Smith was his prophet, that the Book of Mormon was true. He knew it other than by hearsay. Then, when he closed his testimony, he turned to those ministers and said, 'Which one of you can testify that you know that you have the truth?" After a brief pause, the leader of the group said, *'Well, we hope we are right.'* " (*CR*, April 1968, p. 121.)

Can you imagine the Church sending missionaries to the ends of the earth to testify that we hope we are right, that we hope the Book of Mormon is true, and we hope that Joseph Smith was a prophet of God? True religion embraces hope, but it certainly is not founded on it.

The Prophet Joseph Smith, paraphrasing in poetic form some verses from the vision of the degrees of glory, described the sectarian world in this language:

These are they that came out for Apollos and Paul;
For Cephas and Jesus, *in all kinds of hope*;

For Enoch and Moses, and Peter and John;
For Luther and Calvin, and even the Pope,

For they never received the gospel of Christ
Nor the Prophetic spirit that came from the Lord;
Nor the covenant neither, which Jacob once had;
They went their own way, and they have their reward.
        —*Times and Seasons* 4:85, italics added

Discussing the principle of revelation in a very astute cri-
tique of what the world calls "Christianity," Thomas Paine
pointed out that "it is a contradiction in terms and ideas to call
anything a revelation that comes to us at secondhand, either ver-
bally or in writing." If, he reasoned, something had been
revealed to one person and not to another, it is revelation to the
first person only. When it is told to a second person and by the
second person to the third and so on, it ceases to be revelation
to those persons. "It is revelation to the first person only and
hearsay to every other, and consequently they are not obligated
to believe it.

"When Moses told the Children of Israel that he received
the two tablets of the commandments from the hands of God,
they were not obliged to believe him, because they had no other
authority for it than him telling them so.

"When I am told that the Koran was written in heaven and
brought to Mohammed by an angel, the account comes too near
the same kind of *hearsay evidence* and *secondhand authority* as the
former. I did not see the angel myself, and therefore I have a
right not to believe it.

"When also I am told that a woman called the Virgin Mary
said, or gave out, that she was with child without any cohabita-
tion with a man, and that her betrothed husband, Joseph, said
than an angel told him so, I have a right to believe them or not;
such a circumstance required a much stronger evidence than
their bare word for it; but we have not even this, for neither Joseph or Mary wrote any such matter themselves; it is only
reported by others that they said so it is hearsay upon hearsay,
and I do not choose to rest my belief upon such evidence."
(*The Age of Reason*, pp. 5-6. Italics added.)

Paine's point is a valid one: there is no salvation in a hearsay religion; it is without power and we are without obligation to believe it. It took Joseph Smith and revealed religion to adequately respond to these arguments. "Search the revelations," said the Prophet, and then "ask your Heavenly Father, in the name of his Son Jesus Christ, to manifest the truth unto you, and if you do it with an eye single to his glory nothing doubting, he will answer you by the power of his Holy Spirit." No longer will you be dealing with a hearsay religion, for as Joseph Smith explained, "You will not then be dependent on man for the knowledge of God; nor will there be any room for speculation." Only in this manner can we learn which of the promises granted in ages past are ours and which are exclusive to the ancient saints. Continuing, he said:

"You, no doubt, will agree with us, and say, that you have no right to claim the promises of the inhabitants before the flood; that you cannot found your hopes of salvation upon the obedience of the children of Israel when journeying in the wilderness, nor can you expect that the blessings which the apostles pronounced upon the churches of Christ eighteen hundred years ago, were intended for you. Again, if others' blessings are not your blessings, others' curses are not your curses; you stand then in these last days, as all have stood before you, agents unto yourselves, to be judged according to your works." (*HC* 1:282-83.)

All scripture testifies that whenever God has had a people he has accepted as his own, he has revealed his will to them. Thus, in the revelation on eternal marriage it was made known to Joseph Smith that all that Abraham received from the Lord he received by revelation, and that those revelations included "promises concerning his seed." The Lord told Joseph Smith that he was a descendant of Abraham and therefore those promises were his also. (D&C 132:29-31.) Nephi gives a classical example of this principle, desiring to "see and hear and know" the things his father had experienced; and knowing that since he had the gift of the Holy Ghost and the Holy Ghost is a revelator, he sought for and received the same spiritual experience as his father. Nephi testified of a God who is the "same yesterday, to-day, and forever," a God who will unfold the mysteries of heaven to those who diligently seek him "as well in these times as in times of old, and as well in times of old as in times to come; wherefore, the course of the Lord is one eternal round." (1 Nephi 10:17-19.)

The scriptures inform us that the testimonies we bear are recorded in heaven. (D&C 62:3.) Those who have properly testified of eternal verities will certainly be honored for having done so; and conversely, those who have testified falsely will be held strictly to account for their perjury. Falsehoods receive no honor in eternal tribunals even when perpetrated in ignorance—there is no salvation in error and untruth.

As a young missionary, Jedediah M. Grant earned quite a reputation for his ability to stand before a congregation and speak extemporaneously. As his reputation grew, a group of people decided to put his abilities to a test. They proposed to give him a text only after he was standing in front of an audience and see if he could adequately develop it. A time and place were agreed upon. The place chosen was a courthouse, and when the appointed hour arrived there was not a seat to be found. Elder Grant was called forward and handed a piece of paper; he unfolded it to find his text—the paper was blank! Without a moment's hesitation Elder Grant began his discourse:

"My friends, I am here today according to agreement, to preach from such a text as these gentlemen might select for me. I have it here in my hand. I don't wish you to become offended at me, for I am under the promise to preach from the text selected; and if any one is to blame, you must blame those who selected it. I knew nothing of what text they would choose, but of all texts this is my favorite one. You see the paper is blank (at the same time holding it up to view). You sectarians down there believe that out of nothing God created all things, and now you wish me to create a sermon from nothing, for this paper is blank. Now, you sectarians believe in a God that has neither body, parts nor passions. Such a God I conceive to be a perfect blank, just as you find my text is. You believe in a church without Prophets, Apostles, Evangelists, etc. Such a church would be a perfect blank, as compared with the Church of Christ, and this agrees with my text. You have located your heaven beyond the bounds of time and space. It exists nowhere, and consequently your heaven is blank, like unto my text." Then Elder Grant proceeded to examine all the basic tenets of the religion of his hearers and, in contrast, to proclaim the principles of the gospel in great power. Impressed both with his discourse and his temporal needs, his audience passed the hat and collected sufficient funds for him to buy himself a new suit, a horse, saddle, and bridle." (Andrew Jenson, *The Latter-day Saints Biographical Encyclopedia* 1:57.)

It is in these basic truths that our faith and testimony must center, for as Alma declared, we cannot exercise faith in things that are not true. (Alma 32:21.) "To the law and to the testimony," said Isaiah, "if they speak not according to this word, it is because there is no light in them." (Isaiah 8:20.)

Paul said that "no man can say that Jesus is the Lord, but by the Holy Ghost." (1 Corinthians 12:3.) Joseph Smith said this should be translated "No man can know that Jesus is the Lord, but by the Holy Ghost." (HC 4:602.) He also explained that no one can receive the Holy Ghost without receiving revelation, for the Holy Ghost is a revelator. (*HC* 6:58.) All valid testimony centers in the principle of revelation as it functions through the medium of the Holy Ghost. There is no other acceptable source. If that knowledge is obtained from some other source or in some other way, the scriptures declare that "it is not of God." (D&C 50:18.)

When Christ asked his apostles, "Whom do men say that I the Son of man am?," Peter bore testimony by the power of the Holy Ghost, saying, "Thou art the Christ, the Son of the living God." Honoring that testimony, Christ said, "Blessed art thou, Simon Barjona: for flesh and blood [meaning mortal man, or the arguments of men] hath not revealed it unto thee, but my Father which is in heaven [hath revealed it unto thee]." (Matthew 16:13-17.) That, of course, is the perfect pattern, for, as Moroni testified, "by the power of the Holy Ghost ye may know the truth of all things." (Moroni 10:5.)

In our day three fundamental truths are essential to a valid testimony: first, that Jesus is the Christ; second, that Joseph Smith is a prophet of God; and third, that The Church of Jesus Christ of Latter-day Saints is the only true and living church on the face of the whole earth. All valid testimony must embrace the spiritual witness that Jesus is the Christ, for "there is none other way nor name given under heaven whereby man can be saved in the kingdom of God." (2 Nephi 31:21.) Nor can we profess to accept Christ and reject the prophets that come in his name. "Whosoever receiveth me, receiveth those, the First Presidency, whom I have sent, whom I have made counselors for my name's sake unto you." (D&C 112:20.) Since Joseph Smith was the prophet who restored to the earth the truth about Christ and the authority necessary to perform the ordinances of salvation, it stands to reason that no one in our day and age could be saved independent of both the knowledge and the testimony that Joseph Smith is a prophet of God, or independent of the church organization wherein the authority to perform those ordinances is found.

As an illustration of this principle, consider this testimony of Brigham Young:

"Permit me, my hearers, brethren and strangers, to say to you, there is not that man that hears the sound of my voice this day, that can say that Jesus lives, whether he professes to be his disciple or not; and can say at the same time, that Joseph Smith was not a Prophet of the Lord.

"There is not that being that ever had the privilege of hearing the way of life and salvation set before him as it is written in the New Testament, and in the Book of Mormon, and in the Book of Doctrine and Covenants, by a Latter-day Saint, that can say that Jesus lives, that his Gospel is true; and at the same time say that Joseph Smith was not a Prophet of God. That is strong testimony, but it is true. No man can say that this book (laying his hand on the Bible) is true, is the word of the Lord, is the way, is the guide-board in the path, and a charter by which we may learn the will of God; and at the same time say, that the Book of Mormon is untrue; if he has had the privilege of reading it, or of hearing it read, and learning its doctrines. There is not that person on the face of the earth who has had the privilege of learning the Gospel of Jesus Christ from these two books, that can say that one is true, and the other is false. No Latter-day Saint, no man or woman, can say the Book of Mormon is true, and at the same time say that the Bible is un-

89

true. . . . If Jesus lives, and is the Saviour of the world, Joseph Smith is a Prophet of God . . . and no man on the earth can say that Jesus lives, and deny at the same time my assertion about the Prophet Joseph. This is my testimony, and it is strong." (*JD* 1:38.)

There is no value in a testimony without works to evidence its truth. Valid testimony is always manifest in actions. The test of profession is in the fruits it bears. We cannot have the testimony that Jesus is the Christ without some observable influence in our life. James taught that belief in God independent of good works makes one no better than the devils. Joseph Smith amplified this teaching when he stated that to profess a belief in God without the attendant works is to become like the devils. (JST, James 2:19.) The idea that one can have the faith and the testimony that grows out of faith without works originated with Satan himself.

All valid testimonies have certain characteristics in common. First, they center in truth. One cannot bear legitimate testimony to that which is not true. Second, valid testimony will always claim revelation as its source; the things of God are known by revelation and in no other way. Third, valid testimony will have life in itself; it will not be the outgrowth of hearsay or secondhand evidence. Fourth, such testimony will boldly attest that Jesus is the Christ, that Joseph Smith is the prophet of the restoration, and that The Church of Jesus Christ of Latter-day Saints is the only true and living church on the whole earth. Fifth, such testimony will evidence itself by the company it keeps. Valid testimony will always be found sustaining and supporting other principles of truth and evidencing by good works that it is of God. It will always be found sustaining living prophets.

CHARACTERISTICS
OF TRUE REVELATION

All the revelations of God
teach simply this—
Son, daughter, you are the workmanship
of mine hands:
walk and live before me in righteousness;
let your conversations be chaste;
let your daily deportment
be according to my law;
let your dealings one with another
be in justice and equity;
let my character be sacred in your mouth,
and do not profane my holy name
and trample upon mine
authority; do not despise any of my sayings,
for I will not be disgraced.
(Brigham Young.)

Every principle of truth has its counterfeit. Every spiritual experience has been imitated. While the Church was still in its infancy the Lord cautioned the Saints to avoid deception, reminding them that Satan was "abroad in the land" and that "he goeth forth deceiving the nations." (D&C 46:7-8; 52:14.) The Great Imitator does not labor alone in his efforts to confuse and deceive. Of the sources of falsehoods, the Lord said that "some are of men, and others of devils," but both are "an abomination in his sight." (D&C 46:7; JS-H 1:19.) Joseph Smith said that the ignorance of men about the power and influence of delusive spirits was enough to make the devil "shake his sides." "The world," he said, "always mistook false prophets for true ones, and those that were sent of God, they considered to be false prophets." (HC 4:574.) These they abused, imprisoned, killed, or drove into the wilderness to hide "in deserts, and in mountains, and in dens and caves of the earth." (Hebrews 11:38.) The world, he said, prefers knaves, vagabonds, hypocrites, and imposters to prophets; "The Church of Jesus Christ of Latter-day Saints has also had its false spirits." (*HC* 4:580.) Because of these "abominations in the church" that are done in the name of the Lord, he has directed that "every man beware lest he do that which is not in truth and righteousness" before him. (D&C 50:4, 9.)

Every member of the Church has been promised a spiritual gift or gifts. These gifts are given for personal edification and to enable us to reach out and bless the lives of others with greater facility. There are a great diversity of gifts divided among the Saints. One such gift is the gift of the discerning of spirits. (D&C 46:23.) This gift embraces a special spiritual talent or ability to identify that which is spiritually genuine and to detect that which is spiritual sham. Held by many, this gift has been especially promised to those in positions of presidency that they might, in the area of their particular stewardship, insure that the Lord's house remain one of order. In its fullest sense this gift is always held by the president of the Church. (D&C 46:29.)

Along with the gift of discernment, the Lord has established a host of spiritual laws by which we can discern truth from error. These laws, or spiritual absolutes, constitute the standards used to weigh or measure spiritual correctness. Since the scriptures are replete with these laws, they have been designated as the "standard works." The title appropriately implies that they contain the standards by which we discern the "form of godliness" from eternal truths.

The God of heaven is a God of truth and order. He possesses all the attributes of Godliness in their perfection, and as Joseph Smith taught, he "never changes, therefore his attributes and character remain forever the same." Thus we can exercise the same faith in him as have the former-day saints, and expect the same results. (*Lectures on Faith,* p. 46.) This perfectly consistent and unchangeable God has given us the absolute assurance that he will never allow the man who stands at the head of his earthly kingdom to lead the Church astray. We can always follow the prophet with perfect confidence. We have also been given the assurance that we can place that same confidence in the "united voice" of the leading quorums of the Church. Further, as a God of law, he will never depart from the order he has established in manifesting his will to his people through his chosen mouthpiece. Thus all matters that come from God for his people will come through the channels he has appointed. True prophets and true doctrines will always be in harmony with and in subjection to these principles, and salvation never has been nor will be found conditioned on any other principles.

Though the family of truth is large, it is one in which there is perfect unity. One truth is never offensive to another. The spirit that testifies that Jesus is the Christ will never be found calling him "accursed." (1 Corinthians 12:3.) The spirit that directs men to lend a listening ear to the Lord's prophets will never be found justifying them in a course of obstinacy or rebellion against the Lord's anointed. When the Lord calls a man to a work, it would be inconsistent for him to give the revelation for the accomplishment of that work to another. "It is contrary to the economy of God," taught Joseph Smith, "for any member of the Church, or any one, to receive instruction for those in authority, higher than themselves. . . ." (HC 1:338.) Joseph F. Smith suggested that "to seriously contemplate any such idea would be charging the Almighty with inconsistency, and with being the author of confusion, discord, and schism." (JD 24:189.) All that is revealed from the heavens evidences the order of that kingdom. One gospel truth will always sustain another, and the heavens will always comply with the order they have instituted.

The oil of the lamp of revelation is righteousness. The Holy Ghost teaches in the school of the prophets, not in the classrooms of the wicked. All who have been cleansed through the waters of baptism are invited to enter that school. President Harold B. Lee taught this principle by telling of an inactive member who professed a revelation contrary to a decision made by the stake presidency and the high council in a church court. President Lee, who was the stake president at the time, told the man that "fifteen of the best-living men in the stake prayed" and were united on the matter. He then asked his questioner why he supposed it was that a man who was not keeping the commandments got a different answer. The man acknowledged that his answer could not have come from the Lord. "We get our answer," President Lee observed, "from the source of the power we list to obey." (*Stand Ye in Holy Places,* pp. 136-38.) God does not "bring clean things out of unclean men." (Oscar W. McConkie, *The Holy Ghost,* p. 15.)

It is one thing to get a revelation and entirely another to understand that revelation. Paul, counseling Timothy, said, "The Spirit speaketh expressly," indicating that there are occasions when the Spirit speaks without the same degree of "expressness." (1 Timothy 4:1.) "Revelation does not always come with the same force and power," noted Elder Bruce R. McConkie. (*Doctrinal New Testament Commentary* 3:85.) Recording a revelation, Joseph Smith wrote, "Thus saith the still small voice, which whispereth through and pierceth all things, and often times it maketh my bones to quake while it maketh manifest." (D&C 85:6.)

As with all knowledge, the understanding of revealed experiences comes with time and study, and it too must be taught by the Spirit. Speaking of his revealed experiences Nephi said, "My heart pondereth continually upon the things which I have seen and heard." (2 Nephi 4:16.)

The Lord was critical with those anciently who would not understand with their hearts. (Matthew 13:15.) Of the revelations given to our dispensation the Lord said, "I leave these sayings with you to ponder in your hearts. . . ." (D&C 88:62.) True religion must be both felt and experienced. President Lee illustrated with this experience:

"A few years ago a prominent university professor joined the Church. When I asked him to speak before a group of New York businessmen and to explain why he had joined The Church of Jesus Christ of Latter-day Saints, he said to these men, 'I'll tell you why I joined this church. I came to a time in my life when my heart told me things that my mind did not know. Then it was that I knew the gospel was true.'

"When we understand more than we know with our minds, when we understand with our hearts, then the Spirit of the Lord is working upon us.

"I once had a visit from a young Catholic priest who came with a stake missionary from Colorado. I asked him why he had come, and he replied, 'I came to see you.'

" 'Why?' I asked.

" 'Well,' he said, 'I have been searching for certain concepts that I have not been able to find. But I think I am finding them now in the Mormon community.'

"That led to a half-hour conversation. I told him, 'Father, when your heart begins to tell you things that your mind does not know, then you are getting the Spirit of the Lord.'

"He smiled and said, 'I think that's happening to me already.'

" 'Then don't wait too long,' I said to him.

"A few weeks later I received a telephone call from him. He said, 'Next Saturday I am going to be baptized a member of the Church, because my heart has told me things my mind did not know.' " (*Stand Ye in Holy Places,* pp. 92-93.)

The scriptures evidence a greater concern for the heart of man than for the mind of man. Describing the experience the Nephites had with the resurrected Christ as they witnessed him praying to the Father, the scriptures say, "Their hearts were open and they did understand in their hearts the words which he prayed. Nevertheless, so great and marvelous were the words which he prayed that they cannot be written, neither can they be uttered by man." (3 Nephi 19:33-34.) There is a level of understanding in the heart that exceeds that of the mind. Though revelation is granted to both the heart and mind, it is in the heart that the Holy Ghost dwells. (D&C 8:2.)

The scriptures speak of feelings of peace and assurance that accompany association with the Holy Ghost. Those who live worthy of this association have been promised that they might enjoy the constant companionship of that member of the Godhead. (D&C 121:46.) It was not intended that we live on the memory of spiritual experiences, as marvelous as they are, but rather that our association with the Spirit of revelation be ongoing. All spiritual truths are subject to confirmation. (D&C 50:31.) This is not to say that the Lord holds himself obligated to continuously repeat himself, but rather that we are entitled to recurring assurance that the course we are pursuing is approved by him. It was not intended that each of us go his own way, assured that because he has had a spiritual experience he is now saved, or that the light of heaven will always shine on him. The commandment of the Lord is that we meet together often. We

do so to reinspire each other, to remember Christ and his atoning sacrifice, to renew our covenants to serve him, and to renew
our desire to keep his commandments. These are the reasons we
partake of the sacrament. In doing so we receive anew the
promise that in pursuing such a course we may "always have his
Spirit" to be with us. (D&C 20:75-79.)

There is order in the heavens, and the harmony that exists
between heavenly truths always evidences that order. Such principles are never found warring with each other. They march in
unity and mark a certain course. They are offensive to wicked-
ness and offended by it. There are two great tests by which
heavenly principles can always be identified. The first is the test
of truth. As sincere as a man might be, there is no spiritual
growth without truth. One does not grow closer to God
through error. The second great test is that of conduct. Illustrating this principle John said: "He that saith he is in the light,
and hateth his brother, is in darkness even until now. He that
loveth his brother abideth in the light, and there is none occasion of stumbling in him. But he that hateth his brother is in
darkness, and walketh in darkness, and knoweth not whither he
goeth, because that darkness hath blinded his eyes." (1 John 2:9-
11.) Heavenly light will never be found justifying a course of
unrighteousness.

That which professes to be revelation must always be able to
give positive answers to such questions as the following:

1. Does it fall within the recipient's stewardship or right to
know?

2. Does it sustain the Lord's anointed and is it in direct
compliance with the established order of his kingdom on the
earth?

3. Is it subject to the quiet confirmation of the Spirit?

4. Does it lead to righteousness?

That which comes from God edifies and uplifts. The Spirit
of revelation could be described as that influence which makes
bad men good and good men better. The light of heaven brings
nourishment and strength; where it shines, darkness must flee.

SPIRITUAL INDEPENDENCE: A BILL OF RIGHTS

The power is in them,
wherein they are agents
unto themselves.
(D&C 58:28.)

A few years ago a student of mine in a high school seminary class informed me that he was dropping out of school to join the Marines. In response to my question as to why, he said, "Because I am sick and tired of people telling me what to do."

It is rather doubtful that this young man found the independence he was seeking. Like so many others, he was searching elsewhere for that which could come only from within himself. In his vain search he could be likened to an old man hunting for his hat while wearing it on his head.

All spiritual achievement is rooted within the soul. It matters not how long and arduous the journey, the things of the Spirit remain "hidden treasures" until the pilgrimage is directed within. A young woman came to my office ostensibly seeking counsel to save a failing marriage. Asked if she had sought counsel from her bishop and others with whom she should properly seek direction, she said, "Yes, but they all want me to change." She continues to search and her marriage continues to fail.

We were not created to be the toys of circumstances or the puppets of fate. Though we may not control our destiny, we can control ourselves. Within our souls rest both the ability and the power to think our own thoughts, speak our own words, choose our own friends, determine our own attitudes, and do our own works. No one else can save us in the kingdom of God, nor can any other force or influence combine to prevent our salvation without our consent.

In the early history of the Church, many converts who joined with the body of the Saints expected to find a spiritual utopia. Frustrated at finding that the communities of the Saints were populated with people who in many instances were no better than themselves, some of these immigrants voiced their disillusionment and left the Church. These people had anticipated a Zion in which they could bask in spiritual light day and night. Longing to be nurtured by revelations, miracles, and manifestations of divine power, they sought heaven on earth. They did not realize that spiritual maturity often comes slowly and that many, like themselves, had gathered with the Saints in the hope that there they too might find the courage and strength necessary to overcome their own weaknesses.

Of such people, Brigham Young would inquire, "What hinders you from enjoying all that you anticipated?" If you are not as you desire to be, if you do not feel the promptings or influence of the Holy Ghost to the extent that you think you should, where is the fault to be found? Responding to his own question, President Young explained that it was a mistake to suppose that others could prevent you from enjoying the light of God in your soul. "All hell," he said, "cannot hinder me from enjoying Zion in my own heart, if my individual will yields obedience to the requirements and mandates of my heavenly Master." (*JD* 1:311.)

Brigham Young declared himself to be the only man in heaven, on earth, or in hell responsible for Brigham Young. Further, he held that the same doctrine applied equally to every Latter-day Saint. Salvation is an individual matter. "I am the only person that can possibly save myself," said Brigham. We cannot pin our faith on someone else's sleeve. No one can accept or reject salvation in behalf of another. It is not the object or design of the gospel to create spiritual dependence.

Of those who constantly suspend their own judgment to lean upon others they suppose to have greater wisdom than themselves, President Young said that they "will never be capable of entering into the celestial glory, to be crowned as they anticipate; they will never be capable of becoming Gods." They cannot rule themselves, let alone give direction to others. Spiritually, he likened them to children who need direction in every trifle. "They cannot control themselves in the least, but James, Peter, or somebody else must control them. They can never become Gods, nor be crowned as rulers with glory, immortality, and eternal lives." "Who will?" asked President Young, "Those who are valiant and inspired with the *true independence of heaven*, who will go forth boldly in the service of their God, leaving others to do as they please, determined to do right, though all mankind besides should take the opposite course." (Ibid, p. 312.)

As is the case with all gospel principles, the doctrine of individual accountability grows out of the atoning sacrifice of Christ. Teaching these principles, Nephi testified that we are saved by grace, but only "after all we can do." (2 Nephi 25:23.) It is by the grace of Christ that we have granted to us the materials of life with which we can build, but God does not do the building for us. The responsibility of building with those materials is ours. The plan of salvation is in a large measure a do-it-yourself project.

We could no more expect to be saved by the efforts of others than we could expect a meal eaten by someone else to satisfy our hunger. When Christ instructed us to pray for our daily bread, he did not have in mind that we would then sit under the shade of a tree or on a rock in the desert waiting for the angels of heaven to deliver it. Our faith must correspond with our works. God can bless our crops but we must plant the seeds. Brigham Young said that he would just as soon go to a graveyard and labor to raise the dead as to attempt to bless a people who would not do for themselves all that was within their power. If the sick were to seek a blessing at the hands of the priesthood when simple home remedies were available to cure them, then President Young wondered why they did not let the Lord plant and harvest their crops also. (*JD* 4:24-25.)

The doctrine of individual accountability in no way negates the role of the Church, for it is only within the Church that the ordinances of salvation can be performed. In addition to these saving ordinances, it is through the living oracles and priesthood channels operating within the Church that the course we are to pursue is marked out. Further, the Church provides the social structure for sharing spiritual talents and carrying the gospel message to all the people of the earth. Arguments against the need for constant activity in the Church are at best threadbare.

Some argue that it would be hypocritical for them to be active until they have conquered their sins. Such reasoning is reminiscent of the old man who resolved not to go into the water until he had learned how to swim. Others profess no need for the Church. In their reasoning they begin to sound like a blind man analyzing color. They "just do not see anything in it." Nor will they until they choose to open their eyes to it.

As the resolve of a man is strengthened by the support of his wife, so the faith of the Saints is increased by unity. The scriptures direct that "the church meet together often" (D&C 20:55, 75), simply because there is strength in unity that is not had otherwise. The principle is illustrated in the ordinance of administering to the sick. When there are sick among us, we have been directed to call upon the elders, who are to anoint the sick with oil and bless them. (James 5:14-15.) The reason we call for the *elders* instead of *an* elder is that the union of their faith grants them greater confidence before the Lord than is generally had individually. Thus the Lord said, "Where two or three are gathered together in my name, there am I in the midst of them" (Matthew 18:20)—not because we cannot associate with his Spirit individually, but because our faith increases more rapidly in association with people of like faith than it does in isolation.

The government of heaven is founded on the principle of agency. There is no greater advocate of self-direction than our Heavenly Father, who bequeathed the gift of agency to each of his spirit children at the moment of their spirit birth. Never in all the eternities has God violated that agency or granted anyone else the right to do so. Nowhere in history do we find the heavens sanctioning the right of one man to control another. The kingdom of heaven operates "without compulsory means." The powers of that kingdom can only be handled "upon principles of righteousness." The essential principles of government in that kingdom are persuasion, long-suffering, gentleness, meekness, kindness, and pure knowledge. Control, dominion, and compulsion are not citizens of that heavenly society. The exercise of such influences is offensive to the Spirit of the Lord, causes it to grieve, and results in it and all its attendant powers withdrawing from the offenders. (D&C 121:36-46.)

Our earthly society is a competitive one in which one man's victory often means another man's defeat. Even in the classroom, it is a common experience for students to find themselves in competition for a predetermined and limited number of A grades.

Gratefully no such system is operative in the Lord's kingdom. The blessings of heaven are not dispensed according to the bell curve, nor will one man's success ever limit or deter the opportunities of another. Since "God is no respecter of persons" (Acts 10:34), social standing, wealth, intellectual achievement, and physical attractiveness do not call down the blessings of heaven.

Obedience is the common denominator by which all blessings must be sought. So it was decreed and understood long before our birth into this life. (D&C 130:20; 132:5.) It was also understood that none were to be excluded from the possibility of obtaining salvation. (2 Nephi 26:24.) "We believe," Joseph Smith wrote, "that through the Atonement of Christ, all mankind may be saved, by obedience to the laws and ordinances of the gospel." (Article of Faith 3.) As Nephi pointed out, Christ has never asked anyone to depart from him or banned anyone from his houses of worship. He has not said to anyone that he could not partake of his salvation. "All men," Nephi testified, "are privileged the one like unto the other, and none are forbidden." (2 Nephi 26:25-28.)

A multitude of ideologies vie for our allegiance. Campaign promises are legion. Zealous and articulate recruiters marching under a host of banners wage a war with words for our support. Give no thought to avoiding the battle, for it is over us that they contend. Their weapons include the sophistry of modern advertisement, which in this unlimited warfare knows no bounds. Strength is promised through effortless routines, freedom is offered in the form of irresponsibility, and salvation is granted by the mere asking. We are offered a seemingly endless parade of panaceas to an equally inexhaustible array of needs. In the midst of this "tumult of opinions," we are left to ask as did Joseph Smith, "Who of all these parties are right; or, are they all wrong together? If any one of them be right, which is it, and how shall I know it?" (JS-H 1:10.)

Of this we can be certain: changing the name of an action cannot change the effect of that action. You can plant corn by any name you choose, but the semantics will never alter your harvest. Lust can be called love, but that which it yields will always be as ugly as the seed from which it sprang. Drugs can be called mind-expanding, but that will not alter the manner in which they wither and shrink both mind and soul. Abandoning the beauty and virtue of womanhood can be called liberation, but having been cut off from its life-giving waters, its fruits sour and rot on the vine. Surrender can be called victory, but its resultant bondage is nonetheless real.

The effects of eternal principles are not supplanted by popular mandate or individual pleading. They apply alike to all men, rich or poor, bond or free. The Church could vote to repeal the Word of Wisdom, the law of tithing, the law of the fast, or any other principle, but such an action could never alter the effects of disobedience to the principle involved. Freedom for both individuals and nations grows only in the seedbed of restraint and self-government. We can no more be without restraint and free than we can be both a Philistine and an Israelite. And though many lay claim to being liberated, the name without the substance is like a well without water; it increases rather than satisfies thirst. Mediocrity often finds refuge in group standards. Significantly, there are no group ordinances in the Church. All covenants are made on a personal basis. It does not matter what *others* believe or do; we will be judged solely on the basis of what *we* believe and do. The folly of group standards is illustrated in the story of the bishop who had five teenage daughters. The time came, much to his consternation, when all five daughters had dates on the same night. The bishop and his wife were concerned because they did not know three of the boys dating their daughters, and even more concerned because they did know the other two. As one would expect prior to the big night, the bishop gathered his daughters around him and reviewed with them church and family standards. He concluded his preachment by announcing the hour at which all of them were expected to be home and informing them that he would be waiting up for them. When the appointed hour arrived, only three of the bishop's daughters had returned home. Quite satisfied, he went off to ready himself for bed. His wife, unable to hide her concern, asked if he was not worried about the two girls who had not returned. "No," replied the bishop, "three out of five are here, and that is sixty percent, which is twice the Church average."

Salvation is not granted on the basis of what others are doing or have done. The scriptural injunction is that we "work out [our] own salvation" (Philippians 2:12) simply because no one else can do it for us.

We do not determine eternal principles nor can we modify them in any way. It becomes our responsibility to take these eternal principles and apply them. Thus, as we personalize gospel verities, we create our own plan of salvation, a plan that honestly recognizes where we are and challenges us to systematically proceed from that point forward, advancing in scriptural language from "grace to grace." The first step in such advancement could appropriately be a personal declaration of independence, one that recognizes that the works that lead to spiritual independence must be our own works; one that recognizes the special rights that are ours as children of God and members of his earthly kingdom. To that end, the following declaration of independence and bill of rights is given.

A Declaration of Independence

As Latter-day Saints we hold these truths to be self-evident: that salvation is available to all men by obedience to the laws and ordinances of the gospel, and that all men are endowed by their creator with certain unalienable rights; that among them are eternal life, spiritual liberty, and the endless pursuit of happiness. That to secure these rights, the kingdom of God has again been established among men, deriving its powers upon principles of righteousness. That whenever any power or influence becomes destructive of these ends, it is the right of the Saints to alter or abolish that influence through faith and repentance and to institute anew their covenant with God, laying its foundation on such principles as to them shall seem most likely to affect their eternal best interest.

A Bill of Rights

I

Obedience to gospel principles produces the same blessings in all ages. Thus we of the latter days are entitled to every blessing enjoyed by the saints in Bible times. The faith that saved men anciently is the faith that saves men today. The faith with which they raised the dead, gave sight to the blind, healed the sick, and cast out devils in the meridian of time is the same faith required to accomplish the same works in our time. The effects of faith are the same for all men in all ages. We have the same claim on that faith and its effects as any other people in any other time, past, present, or future. (1 Nephi 10:17-19.)

II

Having exercised faith, we can, through repentance and baptism, obtain a remission of sins. "Though your sins be as scarlet, they shall be as white as snow; though they be red like crimson, they shall be as wool." (Isaiah 1:18.) Through the divinely appointed process of faith, repentance, and baptism, it is the right of all men to obtain the Lord's promise that he remembers their sins "no more." (D&C 58:42.)

III

Having thus obtained a remission of sins and the attendant peace of conscience, it now becomes our right to associate with the Holy Ghost. By the laying on of hands, the gift of the Holy Ghost is granted. Through this gift comes the right to receive revelation, guidance, light, and truth from the Spirit. The Prophet Joseph Smith said, "No man can receive the Holy Ghost without receiving revelations. The Holy Ghost is a revelator." (HC 6:58.)

IV

The Holy Ghost himself is the giver of gifts and grants to all the faithful special spiritual talents. "All have not every gift given unto them; for there are many gifts," but "to every man is given a gift by the Spirit of God," and all are encouraged to seek earnestly the best gifts, "always remembering for what they are given." (D&C 46:8-11.)

V

All spiritual blessings are predicated upon obedience to laws. (D&C 130:20-21.) Anyone who abides the law receives the blessing. Thus the Lord has said that he is bound when we do what he says, but when we fail to do so we have no promise. (D&C 82:10.)

VI

Bounds and limits in the realm of spiritual things are individually determined. This principle holds true for all attributes of godliness. Spirituality is not an office. Faith is not an office. Knowledge is not an office. Wisdom is not an office. The attributes of godliness are not dependent upon calls to serve; they are not necessarily associated with age; nor are they the province of men or the exclusive inheritance of women. Spiritual strength comes from works of righteousness.

VII

The ability to do good and bring to pass much righteousness has been granted to all men. Inasmuch as they do this, "they shall in nowise lose their reward." (D&C 58:27-28.)

VIII

As members of the Church we are "no more strangers and foreigners, but fellowcitizens with the saints, and of the household of God; And are built upon the foundation of the apostles and prophets, Jesus Christ himself being the chief corner stone." (Ephesians 2:19-20.) Our citizenship in God's earthly kingdom entitles us to the inspired direction of leaders who have drunk deeply of the waters of inspiration and who invite us to partake of the same. At their hands we receive blessings of comfort and counsel, blessings foreshadowing the future, administrations when sick, and special blessings of protection. By faithfully following their counsel, we have been granted the promise that the gates of hell will not prevail against us and that the Lord God will disperse the powers of darkness from before us and cause the heavens to shake for our good and his name's glory. (D&C 21:6.)

IX

Through worthiness we are entitled to enter into the house of the Lord and there be endowed with knowledge, power, and blessings from on high. In the temple, a husband and wife are sealed together for time and eternity, thus preserving the family unit throughout the worlds to come.

X

All faithful Saints are entitled to the assurance that the course they are pursuing is approved by God. To this end, the Holy Ghost grants the promise that "all covenants, contracts, bonds, obligations, oaths, vows, performances, connections, associations, or expectations" will be of "efficacy, virtue, or force" in the world to come. (D&C 132:7.)

The testimony of the angel heralding the birth of Christ was that the good tidings and great joy of the gospel were for all people. (Luke 2:10.) In like manner, Peter testified of a God who was "no respecter of persons." (Acts 10:34.) The promises are ours; they span the ages! "God is not the God of the dead, but of the living." (Matthew 22:32.) The powers of the heavens are not bowed with age and constrained in movement. As men were blessed anciently, they can be blessed today.

Nor do we speak of blessings reserved for apostles and prophets, for there are none such. Joseph Smith taught that "the Lord will not reveal anything to Joseph that he will not reveal to the Twelve or to the least and last member of the Church as soon as he is able to bear it." (Bruce R. McConkie, "Are General Authorities Human?") "Blessings come because of obedience and personal righteousness, not because of administrative positions." (Bruce R. McConkie, *CR,* October 1977, p. 49.)

The understanding and assurance we seek is rightfully ours and will be ours as we desire it, seek after it, and live to receive it. Such is the experience of the faithful in all ages.

INDEX

Marines, boy dropped out of school to join, 97

Mary, mother of Christ, 26-27, 62

McConkie, Bruce R., 33, 78

McKay, David O., 17-19

Meditation, 72

Meekness, 45

Men: accountability of, 2-3; should make some decisions for themselves, 79

Ministers who hoped they were right, 84

Miracles: Saints who require, are not in good standing, 14; man asked Joseph Smith to perform, 15-16

Moses: spiritual training of, 34; was slow of speech, 42; wished all his people were prophets, 55

Need to believe, 9

Obedience: blessings depend on, 101, 105; produces same blessings in all ages, 104

Order in the heavens, 96

Paine, Thomas, 85

Patience, 81

Paul, 7-8, 34, 66-67

Pearls, cast not, before swine, 14

Pharisees, 52

Pondering, 72-73, 94

Pratt, Parley P., 43-44

Prayer: true spirit of, 70; receiving answers to, 70-71; for right things, 70-71; reluctance to engage in, 73-74

Priest, conversion of, 94-95

Proof is not our responsibility, 8-9

Prophets: God calls and educates, 33; spiritual training of, 34; selection of, 63; will never lead the Church astray, 92-93

Questions, asking right, 71

Religion: centers in feelings, 8; embraces but is not founded upon hope, 84

Revelation, 68; men challenged to imitate, 3-4; being sensitive to, 6; spirit of, 39, 72; of three degrees of glory, 39-40; received in answer to questions about Bible, 41-42; must not exceed man's ability, 49; needs to be constant, 51; continuous, rejected by Pharisees and Sadducees, 52; forms of, 53; comes line upon line, 61; test of, by examining its purpose, 68; study and prayer precede, 72; concerning already revealed truth, 80-81; is, by definition, firsthand, 85; personal, 86; depends on righteousness, 93-94; varying degress of, 94; identifying true, 96

Richards, LeGrand, 84

Rigdon, Sidney, 40, 42-43

Sacrament, 96

Sadducees, 52

Saints should not require signs, 13-14

Salvation: Christ worked out his own, 48; requires revelation, 51; individual nature of, 97, 98, 103; ordinances of, 99

Samuel, 63-64

Satan: is Christ's enemy, 10; offers counterfeits to truth, 91

Scriptures, Christ taught from, 29

Sectarian world, poem about, 84-85

Seed of faith, 11

Self, spiritual achievement depends on, 97, 98-99

Signs: wicked generation seeketh, 15; come only by faith, 16-17

Signs of the times, discerning, 1-2

Sins, remission of, 104

Smith, Hyrum, 30, 75